GOVERNANCE AND
AUTHORITY IN THE
ROMAN CATHOLIC CHURCH

GOVERNANCE AND AUTHORITY IN THE ROMAN CATHOLIC CHURCH

BEGINNING A CONVERSATION

Edited by
Noel Timms and Kenneth Wilson

Published in Great Britain in 2000
Society for Promoting Christian Knowledge
Holy Trinity Church
Marylebone Road
London NW1 4DU

The authors and publisher acknowledge with thanks permission to use
material from the following;

M. Hornsby-Smith (1989), *The Changing Parish: A Study of Parishes, Priests
and Parishioners After Vatican II* © Taylor and Francis Books Ltd
J. G. Vaillancourt (1980), *Papal Power: A Study of Vatican Control Over Lay
Catholic Elites* © John Wiley & Sons Limited
T. J. Reese, *Inside the Vatican: The Politics and Organization of the Catholic Church.*
Copyright © 1996 by the Woodstock Theological Seminary.
Reprinted by permission of Harvard University Press.

Biblical quotations are from *The Jerusalem Bible* © 1966 by
Darton, Longman & Todd Ltd and Doubleday and Co Inc.

British Library Cataloguing-in-Publication Data

A catalogue record for this book is available from the British Library

ISBN: 0–281–05251–4

Typeset by Wilmaset Ltd, Birkenhead, Wirral
Printed in Great Britain by
The Cromwell Press, Trowbridge, Wilts

CONTENTS

THE CONTRIBUTORS

David Barker is recently retired as Chief Executive of the Derwent Charitable Consultancy in London, which specializes in advisory services to churches and charities.

Terence Connor is currently Chair of British Agencies for Adoption and Fostering.

Francis Davis retains advisory and trustee roles with several European non-profitmaking organizations and is Managing Director of a leading enterprise in the design and print industry.

Dr Jack Dominian is a consultant psychiatrist (semi-retired), broadcaster, writer and lecturer. He is currently Chairman of ONE plus ONE.

Michael Hornsby-Smith is Emeritus Professor of Sociology at the University of Surrey.

Sarah Lindsell is Chief Executive of Guildford Action for Community Care, a charity concerned with the needs of people on low incomes.

Sister Mary Linscott belonged to the British Province of the Sisters of Notre Dame de Namur. She was also a Chevalier de l'Ordre National du Mérite, in recognition of her services to religious at the levels of both the local and the universal Church. Sister Mary died in 1999.

Fr Enda McDonagh is a priest of the Archdiocese of Tuam, Ireland, and is currently Chair of the Governing Body of University College, Cork.

Fr David McLoughlin is Chaplain and Lecturer of Newman College, Birmingham, and a guest lecturer at Birmingham University.

Fr Robert Ombres OP is now a member of Oxford University's theology faculty and teaches canon law and moral theology.

Kenneth Wilson is the Director of Research at The Queen's Foundation for Ecumenical Theological Education, Birmingham.

INTRODUCTION

It is widely recognized that the twentieth century has lost any clear sense of the source of authority. While traditional sources are being questioned a new source has still to emerge. The result is conflict between those competing to exercise authority and a consequent vacuum at the heart of our communities: the damage to all concerned is destructive of both hope and trust. Regrettably, this situation obtains in both church and state.

The focus of this book is the Roman Catholic Church in which the question of authority is the subject of enduring concern and sometimes fruitful debate and enquiry. The purpose of the book is to facilitate the movement 'from confrontation to conversation.'[1]

Governance and Authority in the Roman Catholic Church is based upon papers delivered to a widely representative group of 50 Roman Catholics, a number of them in the ordained ministry, at Darwen (Lancashire) in November 1997. We were concerned to 'follow the conversation' in the sense of exploring personal concerns and the anxieties of particular communities in the context of serious theological study and its practical application in the light of Scripture, tradition and reason. Thus we were not working to a prepared agenda beyond the delivery of commissioned papers and their subsequent discussion.

The context of the Darwen meeting had been prepared by a working party which had come together under the auspices of The Queen's Foundation for Ecumenical Theological Education in Birmingham. The members of the working party had themselves worked in a similar way to that delineated above and had additionally received a number of communications in which individuals shared their experience of authority as exercised in the Roman Catholic Church today.

The principal focus of the material presented here is the exploration of specific problems facing the Roman Catholic Church in the twentieth century. Enda McDonagh, for example, argues that 'plurality and ambiguity are nowhere more rampant than in the experience of Church'. Thus he explores several models of 'church' and various forms of relationship, for example that between the local bishop and the increasingly centralized authority of Rome and various ways in which the matter of secular participation in church governance may be explored. Such complex issues have historical, theological and sociological roots and the difficulties implicit within them are by no means unique to the Church: everyone is affected by the speed and scale of social change. It is, however, important to keep in mind that the Church is required to be informed by Scripture, tradition and reason, and the way in which it tackles the problem it faces will, hopefully, inform the way in which it can best help others.

Jack Dominian and Michael Hornsby-Smith deal with the experience of authority in the Church from a psychological and sociological perspective. Dominian takes the view that the obedience of Christ to the Father is based exclusively upon love and contrasts this with the model currently assumed by those of responsibility resulting from a confident maturity. Hornsby-Smith deals with that arbitrary style of clerical governance which frustrates the independent and authoritative expression of the non-ordained and frustrates the 'democratic imperative'. Terry Connor and Sarah Lindsell argue that while the Church is not a democracy it must be accountable, more particularly because it is a 'voluntary organization'. While this is by no means an attempt to impose management theory upon the Church, Connor and Lindsell stress the fact that precisely because the purpose of the Church is 'service' those in authority need to be seen to *serve* in order to free the Church as a whole to fulfil this role.

David McLoughlin explores 'service in communion' in a study of the role of a local bishop. The apparent coexistence in the Church of two supreme authorities requires investment in dialogue so that church practice may reflect a Trinitarian theology whereby the desirable unity is maintained by the unity of reciprocal relations. Robert Ombres discusses the fact that secular involvement in 'collaborative ministry' presents particular problems for the Roman Catholic Church because of the current requirements of canon law.

He emphasizes that these requirements have varied over the centuries and that recent codification would seem to have brought clearer and more precise definition of certain aspects. With regard to the assumed bond between holy orders and jurisdiction, Ombres suggests that in the area of lay ministry not everything that has happened in history establishes tradition in its correct theological sense nor should it be repeated in different circumstances.

David Barker argues that the Church is trying to reduce the problems it faces by regulation, definition and codification but that such an approach will inevitably lead to conflict in terms of unresolved tension resulting from differing interpretations of the requirements of the Second Vatican Council and increasing complexity at the level of parish and diocese.

Enda McDonagh's point is that one of the more valuable results of Vatican II was its acknowledgement of the rich medley of metaphors and models of church already in use in New Testament times.

In contrast Francis Davis suggests that the Catholic world is in fact composed of 'organizations and images' – some of them extremely opposed to one another and, indeed, mutually exclusive in orientation. He observes that differing images of church may in fact be rooted in differing theories about life and differing notions of God.

However, far from being destructive, such variation in fact presents a marvellous opportunity for the encouragement of a truly 'catholic' church in a time of rapid change. It is thus appropriate that Kenneth Wilson reviews the question of authority and governance in a wider ecumenical context.

The issue of women in the Church is addressed broadly rather than in terms of ordination alone. Mary Linscott enlarges upon the intriguing lessons to be learned from the responses of women religious to the Second Vatican Council in that the question of authority and governance quickly became 'live' for women's congregations from 1966.

In a concluding paper David Barker develops the question of authority and governance in the Church in a broader societal context in order to continue the conversation.

It is our sincere hope that the discussion thus engendered will not only extend further within the Roman Catholic Church but will extend to other churches as well as to those concerned with similar issues in society. For St Thomas, the chief end of human life is to know and love God who is the goal of human life. It is in this spirit that we invite your response to the issues raised in this book.

Noel Timms
Kenneth Wilson

Note

1 The title of the first discussion paper prepared for the working party.

Chapter One

FOR THE LOVE OF GOD: THE ROLE OF AUTHORITY IN FAITH

Jack Dominian

Dr Jack Dominian was born in Athens and educated in India and Great Britain. He qualified as a doctor in 1955 and as a psychiatrist in 1961. He was Senior Consultant Psychiatrist at Central Middlesex Hospital for 25 years, and took a special interest in marriage and sexuality. He has written several books on the subject of marriage and the relationship between psychology and religion. In 1971 he set up the Marriage Research Centre, which is now called ONE plus ONE.

Introduction

This chapter argues that after a relatively brief glimpse of an alternative disposition encouraged by the Second Vatican Council the Church has relapsed into a mode of existence which assumes the immaturity of the faithful. In the first section, three psychological theories are briefly reviewed to illustrate a crucial distinction between a primitive, early obedience which is absolute and unilateral and a developed evaluative obedience of a more mature character. The theories can also illuminate ways in which the Church has related to its people and vice versa. The second section suggests that the mature mode of obedience can be centred on the person and the experience of Christ.

Psychological Theories of Moral Development

FREUD

I start with Freudian theory because amongst psychological theories it is the oldest and best known. Freud postulated that our personality is shaped by the two instinctual drives, the sexual or Eros and the aggressive. He further postulated that the energy of these two drives lies in a part of the mind called the id, whose aim is

1

the fulfilment of these drives; opposed to this pleasure principle is the conscious function of the ego, which assesses what is possible according to the reality principle. Reality is the world that is possible given our social, emotional and physical constraints. So far so good. Two forces opposing each other and action being seen as the compromise between the two.

Freud did not stop there, however. He suggested that in addition to the id and the ego, there was a third mechanism called the super-ego. This is a largely unconscious function (though parts are conscious) by which the authoritative commands, injunctions and prohibitions of parents, teachers and figures of authority are taken in and stay alive so that when these are violated a feeling of guilt is engendered. This is how Freud explains our discomfort on breaking some rule which we have long ago abandoned on rational grounds. We all know how uncomfortable we feel when we do something prohibited in our childhood, or how difficult we find it to discard rules that we clearly see are no longer relevant in our life.

I am not saying that the superego is exactly the same as conscience, but there are similarities between the two. We can see the truth in the Jesuit view that it is early years that soak up the most basic teachings, both positive and negative, which instil responses in later life. Independent of the specific rules and regulations that are taught, we respond to authority in these early years with reflex obedience which leaves a mark on our character. This is a powerful mechanism, and the pre-conciliar Church could govern most efficiently on such a principle.

PIAGET

Cognitive theory, which owes its origins to the Swiss psychologist and research worker Piaget, starts from a very different viewpoint to that of Freud. Not feelings but intellectual development is treated as the principal constituent of personality development. The faculty of knowing is the key to human growth and this theory fits in with the traditional emphasis in the educational world on intelligence and the intellect. Cognitive growth, however, takes place concurrently with emotional development and to ignore the one or the other militates against the concept of human wholeness. There is little doubt that this is precisely what has happened in Western educational thought, which has excessively emphasized the intellectual against the emotional.

Up to the age of seven the child, according to Piaget, knows the world only as he physically sees, hears and touches it through words and appropriate signals. As a result he expects everyone to understand him without his having to explain himself. This unity between object, action and thought, which continues until the age of concrete operation, has a special application to obedience. Father, mother and figures of authority are objects whose rules and commands are absolute. Once their special position has been accepted, and this is virtually automatic for all children, obedience is blind and has no differentiating features. Obedience means being good and is absolute whilst disobedience is absolutely bad. There is no hierarchy of values. Breaking rules is also simple. Intention does not come into the life of the child in these early years. Everything is assessed by sheer quantity. The amount of lying, damaging, disobeying is what matters. The underlying reasons for actions or extraordinary circumstances are not considered. Punishment follows closely on these beliefs and is proportional to the gravity of the misdeed, once again regardless of the underlying circumstances. The child expects automatic punishment as a form of expiation which accompanies immanent justice; that is to say it is the subject himself who delivers a verdict of guilty and expects punishment automatically every time he does something wrong. Such is the morality of the young child. Piaget calls it moral realism. Moral rules are external to the child, totally related to authority; punishment has to be literal, automatic and regardless of circumstances.

One can see that much of the thinking of authoritarian figures on obedience, discipline and punishment relies on this early pattern. This is not surprising. It is one of our earliest experiences and we are therefore heavily conditioned to it. We return to it in all conditions of danger. The discipline of an army is very much like it and we accept it at times of disturbance and war. We drop into such automatic discipline and obedience at all times of danger such as those associated with accidents on motorways, outbreaks of dangerous diseases or even in the acute phase of an illness when we obey the orders of a nurse or a doctor unquestioningly. In all these situations we abrogate our judgement, we hand ourselves over to others. Such a situation means that human beings can be managed with the least amount of interference from private judgement, decision or reciprocity.

Turning to the Church, we may see advantages in this blind and automatic obedience to authority. What is not appreciated in this model is that the level of maturity present in such a response is appropriate to the early years of life, and so the Church could be regarded as an organization which encourages immaturity in its members. But it does not have to be so. Piaget found that this level

of moral realism changes into a morality of cooperation and reciprocity in the older child. Children can order their experiences, not independently of others, but in relation to them. They see themselves
as capable of independent thought but now recognize that this is a
process of which others are also capable. Relationships of reciprocity with peers begin around about the age of seven.

There is then a significant shift from *unilateral* respect, hitherto addressed to parents and figures of authority, to *mutual* respect. The
child's capacity for independent thinking also means that he is
aware of himself and others in a more autonomous manner. Rules
cannot be changed arbitrarily and unilaterally. Agreements are
mutual and have to be respected. This sense of equality which first
appears with peers inevitably extends to parents and figures of
authority, a process which is well on the way by the end of the first
decade of life.

The stage of development from unilateral to mutual respect, from
a morality of realism to a morality of reciprocity, is crucial for any
discussion of faith, obedience and morality in the Christian community. It is no exaggeration to say that the tension in the Church at
the present moment can be seen in terms of the psychology that
separates the first seven years of life from subsequent years.

Learning Theory

Neither Freud nor Piaget aimed at describing the ways in which
human behaviour is actually acquired, maintained or changed.
For this we need a third psychological theory, learning theory,
which is associated with Pavlov, Hull, Skinner and Eysenck.

Everyone is familiar with Pavlov's classic experiments with his
dogs. By studying a simple physiological activity like salivation, he
showed that new experiences can be learned. It is an ordinary observation, both in animals and human beings, that in the presence of
hunger, salivation occurs to a greater extent when the promise of
food is at hand. In what has now become standard terminology the
food is the stimulus and the salivation is the response. Thus there is
formed, according to the learning theory, a stimulus–response
bond. There are thousands of situations in life in which the stimulus–response bond exists, of which the red traffic light and stopping
the car is a common example.

To the young baby the face of mother is the stimulus to comfort,
reassurance, food or being picked up. In this way associations are
formed throughout our lives on the basis of required gratification,
or more technically, reduction of drive. Learning theory or behavi-

ourism is not concerned with emotions or intellectual processes. It is the least complicated of the three theories in that it simply describes what happens in practice.

We can now consider human growth on the basis of learning theory. For this we turn to the work of Sears, who has tried to combine psychoanalytic insights with learning theory. For him, the key experience of the child is dependency on parental figures, principally the mother, for meeting its needs. It is she who supplies food, and is therefore the sources of closeness, touch, warmth – powerful signals of comfort, security and love. A child in fact is utterly dependent on mother for food, warmth, support, reassurance and security, and on this is established a whole sequence of learning responses. No one doubts that these habits, learned in the presence of mother, teach us how to please and placate and therefore elicit responses of approval and love. These form the basis, the infrastructure, of all future behaviour in circumstances when we want similar responses.

Now traditionally the Church has been considered a spiritual mother whose approval we elicit. Our dependency on her for our salvation is a powerful psychological factor. There is an inbuilt desire to please by conforming.

But, as is commonly known, the dependency needs of the child are opposed by those of autonomy which occur very early on, indeed as far back as the second year of life. Here then is a classic and recurrent human drama. We require approval, affection and love from another person, which means pleasing them, doing things their way, and yet we wish to do things our way to retain our autonomy, not to become simple extensions of the other person. The tension between dependence for approval and autonomy is acted out in the life of the Church. In the past there was the additional complication that the Church held the key to eternal salvation, and fear of eternal punishment played a large part in the minds of many. To displease was to incur the risk of not only temporal disapproval but the eternal loss of one's soul.

The Practice and Experience of Christ

The bonds which held society together in the pre-industrial period were primarily intimate, linked with the family and the fact that those responsible for production and consumption of essential goods were also in close proximity to each other. The advent of industrialization and urbanization had progressively severed these bonds, increasing anonymity and impersonality. The ensuing lack of cohesion was camouflaged by authoritarian structures which remained widespread in industry, business, the professions and society in general. These were extensions of the parent–child dependence patterns of the early years of childhood, translated in adult life into economic, emotional and social dependence, backed by sanctions of fear, awe and guilt.

Christianity has participated in this social evolution and has, in my opinion, singularly failed to promote the principles of the kingdom of God which have Christ and love at their centre, but instead has relied on the same authoritarian structures as the rest of society to underpin the development of the Good News. This has been an error of major dimension, so that in our century when these authoritarian structures are being increasingly attacked and altered, the faith of Christians has been severely undermined in so far as it has rested on the shifting sands of authority and not on the rock of Christ himself.

Christ's Relationships with His Father

What is the authority of Christ? I argue that although Jesus lived under the authority of his parents, by the age of twelve he had managed to achieve a sufficient degree of separation from them to know that his identity was fundamentally linked to his relationship with his Father, without rejecting his earthly parents. This relationship with his Father is the key to all his authority. Christ is obedient to the will of his Father, but it is not the obedience which is consequent on the inequality, immaturity or dependence which are the characteristics of early childhood. There is no inequality of worth.

'The Father and I are one.'

(John 10.30)

There is no immaturity in the sense of lacking fullness or wholeness.

'I am the way, the truth and the life.'

(John 14.6)

There is no dependence in the sense that Christ lacked anything essential for being.

'For the Father, who is the source of life,
has made the Son the source of life.'

(John 5.26)

'Everything the Father has is mine.'

(John 16.15)

The relationship to the Father was one of utter equality in the presence of differentiating roles as persons of the Trinity. But what then is the basis of the obedience if not on any characteristic of inequality? On the answer depends the whole Christian understanding of relationship, authority and obedience.

Christ's relationship of obedience to the authority of His Father was based on that of love and on absolutely nothing else. This was the love that Christ knew the Father had for Him, to which He responded freely and without any sense of compulsion or coercion.

> 'The Father loves me, because I lay down my life
> in order to take it up again.
> No one takes it from me; I lay it down of my own free will.'

> (John 10.17–18)

St John's Gospel makes it very clear how intimately linked obedience and love are in Christ's life, and therefore how the Christian contribution to authority most be totally concentrated on this reality, in which obedience to God is exercised in and through love and for no other reason.

The obedience of love from Son to Father is often portrayed theologically as the symbol of absolute obedience required and owed to God. In my view this is a mistaken theological concept. The obedience in fact arises out of the certainty of the relationship of love which the unity of Father and Son established. Christ wants us to love the Father as he loves him.

> 'May they all be one. Father, may they be one in us,
> as you are in me and I am in you,
> so that the world may believe it was you who sent me.
> I have given them the glory you gave to me,
> that they may be one as we are one.
> With me in them and you in me,
> may they be so completely one that the world will realise
> that it was you who sent me
> And that I have loved them as much as you loved me.'

> (John 17.21–3)

The kingdom of God is about eternal life, and eternal life, according to John, is concerned with the acknowledgement of Jesus Christ, and through him the Father, through the sharing of love which is the foundation of Christ's relationship to the Father.

Christ and the Meaning of Love

There can be no doubt that Christ made a deep impression on those around him because as Matthew tells us,

> He taught with authority, and not like their own scribes.
>
> (Matthew 7.29)

How was this authority revealed in and through love? The authority of love or the love in his authority is to be manifested first and foremost in service.

> 'You know that among the pagans their so-called rulers lord it over them, and their great men make their authority felt. This is not to happen among you. No; anyone who wants to become great among you must be your servant, and anyone who wants to be first among you must be slave to all. For the Son of Man himself did not come to be served but to serve, and to give his life as a ransom for many.'
>
> (Mark 10.42–5)

Service is the key to authority. Service means personal availability and the authority of Christ; indeed every Christian is to be identified in the rendering of service which makes the self available to others.

Personal availability is dependent on wholeness. We cannot give to others what we do not possess ourselves. Availability depends on the greatest possible development of our own wholeness. Man is a unity of his physical, psychological (including intellectual and emotional dimensions), social and spiritual realities. Our wholeness depends on the greatest possible harmonious realization of the conscious and unconscious potential of these realities. The realization of this potential depends on our self-esteem, on the affirmative acceptance of ourselves. There is no point in having the most powerful body or mind or the greatest social aptitude if we feel insignificant, helpless, bad, inadequate or unworthy. We love ourselves through self-acceptance, we love others through making ourselves available to them.

This affirmative availability to others requires, however, another characteristic, namely empathy. Through empathy we are able to become aware of the inner world of another person. The greater our awareness of the inner world of another person, the greater our ability to respond accurately to their mood and physical and emotional needs, to grasp their unexpressed yearnings, to clarify their confusion and to facilitate the emergence of themselves without the intrusion of our interpretation of reality. The difference between advice and counselling is that in the former we care but give a point of view which applies to our own life: in other words, that is how we would act, think or respond in the circumstances before us. In counselling we care by facilitating the appropriate response of the 'other', who acts, thinks and responds in a way that retains his independence, does not become an extension of us, and therefore does justice to his wholeness and integrity.

Christ certainly had this capacity of awareness of what was going on in others, evidence of which, as one might expect, is to be found in the most psychological of all Gospels, namely that of St John.

> During his stay in Jerusalem for the Passover, many believed in his name when they saw the signs that he gave, but Jesus knew them all and did not trust himself to them; he never needed evidence about any man; he could tell what a man had in him.

> (John 2.23–5)

The awareness of others is enhanced if the relationship that ensues is one of equality. Authoritarian philosophy stresses the power of those who have authority and the helplessness of those who do not. This means there is an intrinsic inequality in the status of the two. Those who have power are the givers, with the magnanimity of not needing but simply endowing. When those in authority become angry or their dignity is offended, they have to be mollified or placated. Then they are expected to show mercy and compassion. In relationships of equality much of this hierarchical exchange does not occur. Instead what matters is the fullness of love exchanged.

The sorrow, distress and feelings of badness arise out of the failure to love enough. The need for reparation exists whenever our love has been less than full and the deficiency has hurt or damaged another person by a deed of commission or omission. When we are on the receiving end of such a failure of love, this should not constitute an attack on our dignity, status or significance requiring restitution for such an offence and giving us the opportunity to be merciful and compassionate. Instead what is required is the ability to make it possible for the person who has hurt us to make reparation to us without losing his self-respect. It is no good pretending that we have not been hurt. We can and must acknowledge this, but the hurt is mutual. On our part we have suffered a loss of love, the other has suffered the loss of being a loving person. Our responsibility is to restore, as far as possible, the other's capacity to love.

Christ made it abundantly clear that he related on the basis of equality and friendship.

'This is my commandment: love one another, as I have loved you. A man can have no greater love than to lay down his life for his friends. You are my friends, if you do what I command you.

I shall not call you servants any more, because a servant does not know his master's business; I call you friends, because I have made known to you everything I have learned from my Father.'

(John 15.12–16)

You may say it is all very well describing love in these terms but in a world saddled with sin there are always those who will criticize, attack and even attempt to destroy us. Nevertheless much time and thought has been spent on the theology of a just war and too little on understanding the supreme importance of the Christian message which identifies authority with service and service with availability. There cannot be service or availability in the pursuit of love unless relationships are maintained and not severed. Christianity should not be concerned primarily with the theology of the just war but with the psychology of maintaining viable relationships between persons, groups, nations – indeed one of my definitions of love is staying in relationship.

Christ and the Avoidance of Condemnation

One of the essential features in the maintenance of relationship is to avoid judgements and condemnations. Putting the blame on others is one way of preserving our self-esteem. There are people who can never admit to doing anything wrong. This is not simply stubbornness. Their denial is often genuine. They cannot accept any sense of badness or criticism because their underlying feelings about themselves are already so markedly self-rejecting that conscious admission of their badness will overwhelm their bruised, battered self-image. So all the badness has to be projected on somebody else. It is always somebody else's fault.

If, on the other hand, the person's self-esteem is high, then accepting responsibility is easier because a mistake, fault or bad action will not bring about the destruction of their wholeness. Their sense of goodness is greater than their sense of badness, and so responsibility can be admitted without threatening the security of their whole being. They do not need scapegoats and have nothing to gain from the discomfort of others. They do not need the diminution of others to boost their own significance. Thus they are likely to be slow to judge or condemn others. Jesus said:

'You judge by human standards; I judge no one.'

(John 8.15)

These points are relevant for the authority of the Church, which finds it very difficult to admit it has made a mistake and is forever judging. Nevertheless it is one thing to judge in the sense of condemnation but another to evaluate the deeds and thoughts of others. So what if these are in fact judged to be bad and they do harm us? Here is an important aspect of love, how to remain in relationship with those who have genuinely hurt us, whether consciously and deliberately or by default and unintentionally. In either case what is needed is forgiveness. Forgiveness is essential if we are to stay in relationship with others.

The words of Christ on forgiveness are unbelievably demanding, but they offer the criteria for the life expected in the kingdom of God.

'You have learned how it was said: you must love your neighbour and hate your enemy. But I say this to you: love your enemies and pray for those who persecute you; in this way you will be sons of your Father in heaven for he causes his sun to rise on bad men as well as good, and his rain to fall on honest and dishonest men alike. For if you love those who love you, what right have you to claim any credit? Even the tax collectors do as much, do they not? And if you save your greetings for your brothers, are you doing anything exceptional? Even the pagans do as much, do they not? You must therefore be perfect just as your heavenly Father is perfect.'

(Matthew 5.43–8)

And this loving of one's enemies requires the forgiveness described by Matthew.

Then Peter went up to him and said, 'Lord, how often must I forgive my brother if he wrongs me? As often as seven times?' Jesus answered, 'Not seven, I tell you, but seventy-seven times.'

(Matthew 18.21–2)

Chapter Two

SOME SOCIOLOGICAL REFLECTIONS ON POWER AND AUTHORITY IN THE CHURCH

Michael P. Hornsby-Smith

Michael Hornsby-Smith is Emeritus Professor of Sociology at the University of Surrey. After a period as a lecturer in metallurgy, during which he completed a B.Sc.(Soc.) at London University by part-time study, he subsequently transferred to the sociology department at the University of Surrey where he remained until his retirement in 1998. His numerous publications include *Catholic Education* (Sheed and Ward, 1978), *Roman Catholics in England* (Cambridge University Press, 1987), *The Changing Parish* (Routledge, 1989), *Roman Catholic Beliefs in England* (Cambridge University Press, 1991), and, with John Fulton and Margaret Norris, *The Politics of Spirituality* (Clarendon, 1995). He co-authored *Roman Catholic Opinion* (1979) with Ray M. Lee and edited *Catholics in England 1950–2000* (Cassell, 1999).

Introduction

This chapter reflects from a sociological perspective on the nature of authority in the Church and on styles of governance and ways of exercising authority. It recognizes that such matters are historically contingent and responsive to changes in secular culture, such as a democratic imperative and expectations of participation in decision-making, and considers, in particular, the shifts of theological orientation and emphases occasioned by the Second Vatican Council. A reappraisal of such issues is appropriate as we approach the millennium and consider the ways in which the Church is attempting to redefine its role in the contemporary world.

Challenges to the authority of the Roman Catholic Church and its styles of governing abound in the world of high modernity (Giddens, 1990; 1991) and are no doubt amplified by the globalizing tendencies of modern communications and the possibilities of information technology. The 'authority' of the Church and of its clerical officers has recently been shaken by the well-publicized cases of Bishops Eamonn Casey and Roderick Wright and the reopened debate about compulsory celibacy of the priesthood. In recent years, too, there has been an alarming number of attested cases of child abuse by priests and in Catholic institutions. There is a certain amount of anecdotal evidence of clerical authoritarianism at all levels, sometimes met by overt or covert lay resistance. The ill-fated papal encyclical *Humanae Vitae* (Paul VI, 1968) is widely regarded (e.g. by Greeley et al., 1976) as having shattered the expectations of a more open, 'People of God' model of the Church, as articulated by the Second Vatican Council, especially in *Lumen Gentium* (Abbott, 1966, pp. 14–96; Butler, 1981; Dulles, 1976), in place of an older, more hierarchical model.

Questions of authority and governance in the Church can perhaps best be considered at two main levels. First, the global level and the nature of the relationship between the 'head office' of the Church, that is the Pope and Curia in the Vatican, and the local Churches, in particular the individual bishops' conferences, throughout the world. Second, there are styles of clerical leadership exercised at the local level, such as the Church in England and Wales, or Scotland, or between a diocesan bishop and his priests and lay people, or between a parish priest and his parishioners. There have been tensions and expressions of concern at both levels since the end of the Second Vatican Council in 1965.

At the level of papal leadership there is little doubt that both Paul VI and John Paul II exercised their role in a different way to John XXIII. In his encyclical *Humanae Vitae* Paul VI discounted the advice of John XXIII's Commission on Population, Family and Birth (Kaiser, 1987). Many consider that because of the expectations raised of a change in the Church's teaching about birth control, the rejection of the advice of an expert commission seriously weakened the influence of papal teaching and of the clergy generally, at least in the advanced industrialized nations.

But this was not the only example which appeared to contradict the expectations aroused by the Council. Vaillancourt (1980) has reported how the Vatican manipulated control over the lay elites attending the Third World Congress for the Lay Apostolate in 1967. Significantly, there has been no subsequent World Congress of the Laity and this can be interpreted as an instance where the emergence of a serious and articulated expression of an independent and authoritative lay voice in the Church has been suppressed by the clerical leadership. There are numerous other examples such as the Vatican response to the emergence of progressive tendencies in the Dutch Church with the appointment of conservative bishops in the early 1970s against the wishes of many priests and lay people in their dioceses (Coleman, 1978). Progressive theologians, such as Hans Küng, have been stripped of their official teaching roles, and progressive bishops, such as Helder Camara, have been replaced by conservative traditionalists. Indeed, the strategy of appointing conservative bishops throughout the world has been followed ruthlessly under the present papacy. New movements such as Opus Dei, Focolare and the Neo-Catechumenate have been assiduously promoted and the Basic Christian Community movement, influenced by threatened liberation theologians, strongly discouraged. In all these ways there is clear evidence of strong centralizing tendencies in the way the Church is governed, i.e. its governance (Collins, 1997).

There have also been tensions with styles of governance at the level of the relationships between clergy and laity in the life of the local Church. There are numerous instances of autocratic styles of leadership at the diocesan and parish levels, often without forms of due consultation which the rhetoric about collaborative ministries in the post-Vatican Church (Catholic Bishops' Conference, 1996) would lead one to expect. Instances of this include episcopal pressure on Catholic parents, backed by sacramental or pastoral sanctions, to send their children to a new and poorly attended Catholic comprehensive school, the abrupt scrapping of a diocesan Justice and Peace Commission or of long-standing parish councils, and instances of major and expensive presbytery or parish building projects. It seems that such arbitrary styles of clerical governance are not prohibited by canon law. This matter of the place assigned to the laity by canon law is pursued further in the present collection by Fr Ombres.

Sociological Perspectives

For sociologists it is important to distinguish the power to coerce from the legitimacy attached to an authority, that is 'a person whose opinion is accepted'. They usually take as their starting point Max Weber's treatment of different forms of legitimate domination. Weber distinguished the concept of 'power',

> the probability that one actor within a social relationship will be in a position to carry out his own will despite resistance, regardless of the basis on which this probability exists,

from that of 'authority',

> the probability that a command with a given specific content will be obeyed by a given group of persons.
>
> (1964, p. 152; 1968, p. 53)

This led him 'to classify the types of authority according to the kind of claim to legitimacy typically made by each' (1964, p. 325; 1968, p. 213). In particular he distinguished three types of legitimate authority based on legal-rational, traditional and charismatic grounds (1964, p. 328; 1968, p. 215).

A number of commentators have suggested a 'missing' fourth type of 'value-rational' authority (Willer, 1967; Satow, 1975; Hammond et al., 1978) in Weber's treatment, and others have suggested various elaborations (Harrison, 1960; 1971). Weber anticipated this when he denied that 'the whole of concrete historical reality can be exhausted in the conceptual scheme' which he developed (Weber, 1964, p. 329; 1968, p. 216). Hornsby-Smith (1991, pp. 190–203) has used Weber's categories for an extended consideration of transformations of religious authority in the Church in recent decades.

A number of other conceptualizations in the sociological literature are of value and might be noted briefly. In my view, Burns and Stalker's (1966, pp. 119–22) distinction between a 'mechanistic' or bureaucratic management system which is appropriate to stable conditions and an 'organic' or network type which is appropriate to changing conditions is helpful in interpreting changing styles of governance before and after Vatican II. Etzioni's (1961) comparison between three different types of power and the corresponding types of participant involvement also has relevance for the analysis of clergy–lay relations and lay commitment. Habermas's (1976) analysis of 'legitimation crisis' reminds us that claims to legitimacy of whatever type require justification. In the Church in recent years, there is little doubt that such claims in the realms of sexual morality, the remarriage of divorced people, the rejection of the possibility of women priests, the appointment of conservative bishops against the wishes of local people, and so on, have increasingly been challenged.

Lukes's (1974) distinction between three types of power – to take decisions; to 'mobilize bias' and determine agendas (for example about women priests); and to take on board latent conflicts between parties – has much value. In a recent study of the political culture of American Catholicism, Gene Burns (1996) has drawn on Lukes's analysis and Sewell's (1985) distinction between an ideological core and periphery. This is helpful to the understanding of the marginalization of the Justice and Peace movement (Hornsby-Smith, 1996). Burns also allows us to recognize that some shifts of doctrine occur after political struggles between cultural discourses and he suggests that the increasing rarity of episcopal statements on contraception is an instance of the effectiveness over time of the pressures that the laity can exert on the hierarchy (1996, p. 49). Finally, Gramsci's (1971) concept of hegemony and his distinction between coercive powers and persuasive, hegemonic leadership capable of convincing subordinate groups to follow their advice are also relevant to questions of authority in the Church.

In sum it is suggested that the sociological approach to authority takes as its starting point the nature of the social relationship between the leader and the follower and the nature of response of the latter to the orders or guidance of the former. It takes seriously the distinction between the power to coerce and the authority which a leader has to persuade or induce discipleship or compliance because of a belief in the legitimacy of that leadership. Coercive forms of autocratic leadership do not necessarily have authority and may lead to active rebellion or passive resistance.

In order to understand more fully recent transformations in the nature and scope of religious authority in the Roman Catholic Church and to interpret these changes more completely, the sociologist finds it necessary to situate them in a social and historical context. As far as the Church in England and Wales is concerned, there have been major structural changes since the Second World War. I have discussed these at length elsewhere (Hornsby-Smith, 1987). Lagging somewhat behind the post-war social changes were the religious changes legitimated by the Second Vatican Council. Chief among these was the shift in ecclesiology, the changing self-understanding of the Church in *Lumen Gentium* (Abbott, 1966) as primarily 'the People of God'. Other key concepts were derivative, such as those of episcopal collegiality and lay participation and rights as full members of the Church. Dulles (1976) saw the shift as one from an institutional model of the Church to one which saw the Church as community, sacrament, herald, or servant in the world. The sum total of post-war social and post-Vatican religious changes was the dissolution of the boundary walls which had previously defended a distinctive Catholic subculture (Hornsby-Smith, 1987, pp. 203–17).

For the sociologist it is only to be expected that all these social and religious changes will have changed the nature of social relationships within the institutional Church. Inevitably, the nature of clerical authority and systems of governance will have had to respond to these changes. If we follow Berger, two alternative responses are possible in order to maintain some sort of plausibility in a situation of religious and moral pluralism: intransigence and accommodation (1973, p. 156). There is evidence that both strategies have been employed at different times. Arguably, the whole thrust of the papacy of John XXIII, as reflected in the Second Vatican Council, was to seek an accommodation between the Church and the modern world. In more recent years it has seemed that there has been some reaction and a return to some aspects of a stance of intransigence, for example in the encyclical *Humanae Vitae* of Pope Paul VI (1968) and *Veritatis Splendor* of Pope John Paul II (1993).

The way decision-making is carried out in an organization or social institution may be referred to as the governance of that organization. In the case of the Church it is convenient to distinguish two aspects. In the first place at the macro level, the Church is a major global actor. At this level we might be concerned with the relationships between the Pope and bishops and between the Vatican Curia and national bishops' conferences. Second, at the local level, there are the relationships between the individual bishop and his priests and lay people, and between parish clergy and their parishioners. We will consider each in turn.

Governance in the Global Church

Shortly after the end of Vatican II, Houtart (1968) examined 'critical decisions' and institutional tensions in the Church. He argued that since the Constantinian period, councils have been mainly concerned with organizational issues and that there has been a process of growing centralization in the organization of the Church (pp. 135ff.) and the development of classical bureaucratic values among the Roman Curia. Houtart speculated that Vatican II represented a break with this pattern and the emergence of new patterns of authority at all levels in the Church from the collegiality of the bishops to the birth of bishops' conferences, diocesan pastoral councils and parish councils and the call to responsible participation by all the 'people of God'. The attempt to infuse new values resulted in numerous tensions and conflicts but the attempt to respond to the 'crisis of authority' in an authoritarian way was counterproductive.

In a later paper Houtart examines conflicts of authority in the Church (1969, pp. 319–21). He begins by postulating the existence of contestation in the post-conciliar Church and then attempts an interpretation through the construction of typologies of the objects, types and means of contestation and the official reaction to it. The first object of contestation, according to Houtart, is legitimacy, that is the manner in which authority justifies its function or its decisions. The legitimacy of the authority of the ecclesiastical leadership in the Church has typically been contested over the issues of contraception and clerical celibacy.

The second object of contestation is the value hierarchy proposed or practised by the Church leadership. Thus the values of unqualified obedience or loyalty to religious leaders or their decisions may be contested. It may also be objected 'that these values are contradictory to the evangelical norm, or to the values expressed by the Second Vatican Council' (Houtart, 1969, p. 319). Thus Winter (1973) has contrasted the emphasis on institutional maintenance in the Church with missionary concerns. In a similar vein, some activists contest the low priority given to the issues of justice and peace in pastoral policies and practice and the allocation of resources (Hornsby-Smith, 1996).

Third, Houtart suggests that contestation against the social system or the organizational behaviour of the Church can be identified. Recent examples include

1 Protests against the way the Sacred Congregation for the Doctrine of the Faith pressurizes liberal or liberation theologians (such as Küng, Curran or Boff).
2 The widespread concern within the Church at the cumulative impact of the appointment of traditional bishops against the wishes of the local Church and frequently destroying local initiatives, for example in Holland (see Coleman, 1978) and Brazil.
3 The neglect of human rights in the Church (Sieghart, 1989).
4 Centralizing tendencies in the Church and the erosion of collegiality, for example in the independence of the synods of bishops.
5 The failure to consolidate the enhanced role of lay people in the Church according to the new conciliar 'people of God' theology or to consult them on matters where their knowledge and experience are germane, for instance marriage and family life and the role of women. Active laity in England and Wales pointed to the lack of consultation in the preparation of *The Common Good* (1996; see McGrandle and Jenkins, 1996).

Houtart next distinguishes three *types* of contestation. In the first place *individuals* may contest the teaching or decisions of the ecclesiastical leadership of the Church. It is clear that large numbers of individual Catholics have contested the official teaching on contraception. Second, on other occasions individuals have grouped together to protest. One example was the *Cologne Declaration of European Theologians* (1989) to protest against recent appointments of bishops and constraints on the teaching of theologians. Third, contestation may take the form of a social movement. Examples might include the charismatic movement favouring more spontaneous forms of spirituality; the Basic Christian Community movement, reflecting a greater awareness of the social, economic and political concerns of Catholics in their everyday lives; the justice and peace movement, concerned to raise justice issues to a higher pastoral priority; or recent lay movements in the Church contesting many of the post-Vatican reforms. In a recent example, well over one million people are said to have signed the 'We Are the Church' declaration in Austria and Germany and the movement has now spread to Britain. (See Zulehner, 1996; Bernstein and Politi, 1996, pp. 509–11; and the issues of *The Tablet* for 23 and 30 November, and 7 and 14 December, 1996.)

After distinguishing *individual* or *collective, private* or *public means* used by contestants, Houtart describes three types of reaction to contestation. The religious leadership can unconditionally refuse to accept the contestation through the suppression or exclusion of the individual (e.g. Küng) or group (e.g. the Lefebvrists); or endeavour to limit or diminish the contestation by giving it some legitimation; or they can accept the contestation. It can reasonably be argued that the National Pastoral Congress in 1980 was an attempt to provide a partial legitimation for the concerns of lay people as expressed through numerous groups in preparation for the Congress. On the other hand, the delegates were generally disappointed by the bishops' response to the Congress in *The Easter People* (Anon., 1981, pp. 307–98; Hornsby-Smith, 1987, pp. 36–43) so that in retrospect it seems to have been more an exercise in damage limitation than in acceptance.

Houtart notes that 'where "contestation" has been met positively the result is usually a growth in the moral authority of those who in the Church have a ministerial task' (1969, pp. 320–1) but that otherwise there is the danger of loss of credibility and decay. He postulates that the conflicts in the Church are between two groups of people who assume contrasting models. These two groups perceive authority differently. Traditionalists see authority as a *value*, 'conceived in a vertical way and legitimised by a special divine assistance' while 'progressives' see it as 'a *means* which is more or less efficacious in assuring the pursuit of its goals' (ibid.; emphasis added).

At the apex of the Church's organizational structures stands the papacy, whose traditional authority was underpinned by the doctrine of infallibility. It is appropriate, therefore, that there is at least an embryonic Sociology of the Papacy in two issues of *Social Compass*, Part 1, introduced by Otto Maduro (September 1989) and focusing on the papacy itself, and Part 2 introduced by François Houtart (June 1990) and concentrating on Vatican policies. Of particular interest for our present purposes are two papers examining the papacy of John Paul II. Cadorette (1989) offers a contextual interpretation of the teaching of the Pope during his two visits to Peru in 1985 and 1988 and, in particular, his attack on the liberation theology of Gustavo Gutiérrez which Cadorette claims the Pope has decidedly misinterpreted. Sociologically, it seems that the latent effect of the Pope's attack on liberation theology, pursued by 'strong papal exhortations, pressure exerted by the nuncio against liberal bishops, and a concerted campaign to identify and promote members of the clergy who identify with John-Paul II's neo-conservative definition of Catholicism' (ibid.), is a drastic loss of authority on the part of the Church which acts so as to inhibit the social and structural changes necessary in the pursuit of greater social justice and a loss of 'faith in the Church as a source of meaning and hope' (1989, p. 293).

In the second article, Houtart argues that the visit of the Pope to Nicaragua in 1983 aimed to consolidate the position which the Church had held in civil society before the Sandinista revolution. However, the visit was assessed as a failure and became 'the symbol of unity for a divided opposition, representing the interests of the former ruling social classes; and a critical attitude towards the pope's visit prevailed among the popular classes' (1989, p. 327). A similar critical stance is taken by Dussel in his analysis of eleven major events in the last five centuries of Church involvement in Latin America. Recent Vatican policy, it is argued, has been more concerned with appointments of cardinals who in the next Consistory will elect a conservative pope than with the scandalous situation facing the poor (1990, p. 207).

In his study of *Papal Power*, with a particular analysis of the Third World Congress for the Lay Apostolate, Vaillancourt suggests that:

> the Vatican is, above all, an organisational weapon in the hands of the papacy and other top ecclesiastical officials. Religious ideology has increasingly become subordinated to organisational imperatives. Among these internal and external organisational imperatives, organisational control of lay elites seems to have

become a major preoccupation and necessity for Church authorities. Many Catholic laymen [*sic*] want more autonomy, freedom, and power in all aspects of their lives. They refuse to be passive and obedient members of the clerically dominated Church . . . *It is not authority as such which is rejected, but authority exercised as domination rather than as service and love.*

(1980, pp. 15, 294; emphasis added)

In this section we have looked briefly at governance in the global Church. The problems are immense but there appear to be good grounds for arguing that the current level of organizational centralization is dysfunctional and that legitimacy has been damaged by an insufficient regard for the principle of subsidiarity. This is particularly noticeable historically in the promotion of a European cultural Catholicism and the failure to respond to indigenous forms of religiosity. In the contemporary world, the strategic imposition of conservative bishops on a global scale looks certain to cause widespread alienation of lay people. As Pottmeyer (1996) and Collins (1997) have argued, a reformed Petrine office should be more concerned with achieving consensus through dialogue and with service and collaboration rather than domination.

There remains the contradition of a 'servant Church' being accorded the status of a nation-state in the corridors of world politics and such institutions as the United Nations. Such anomalies are the remnants of the days of the papal states and can only give signals of power and participation in the political games of social control and domination. But, as we have noted, these do not necessarily achieve legitimacy among people generally or guarantee authority in the sociological sense.

Governance at the Local Level

Data relating to governance in the Church at the level of the national church in England and Wales, in the dioceses, and in the parishes is more anecdotal. An example at the national level was the organizational restructuring of the Bishops' Conference and the replacement of the advisory commissions by the present structure of departments and committees which arguably has reduced the opportunities for representatives of lay people to make a contribution to policy-determination. The lack of consultation in the preparation of *The Common Good* incensed lay members of the Catholic Union (McGrandle and Jenkins, 1996), one of three consultative bodies of the Bishops' Conference. Neither the National Council for the Lay

Associations nor the National Board of Catholic Women, the other consultative bodies, had been consulted.

At the diocesan level, Hornsby-Smith et al. (1995) were critical of the top-down nature of a diocesan-wide programme of parish renewal. The disbandment of parish councils, major liturgical alterations, building of new presbyteries, halls or churches without consultation with parishioners, refusals to retain girl altar servers or tolerate women readers or special ministers or give communion in the hand, are all familiar examples of autocratic leadership styles.

In an earlier work I contrasted pre-Vatican and post-Vatican models of the parish priest (Hornsby-Smith, 1989, p. 121). The former was socialized as a 'man apart' with a high premium on obedience, docility and loyalty while the latter was encouraged to a confident flexibility and trained for a co-responsible ministry of service. While relations with lay people were distant in the former case they were close and friendly in the latter. The pre-Vatican priest was authoritarian and the sole initiator in his parish while the post-Vatican priest was a democratic facilitator and enabler. Of course the empirical reality usually falls somewhere between these two models.

> From the relatively meagre research data and impressionistically, it seems to be generally the case that while there is no evidence of serious anti-clericalism in Anglo-Saxon countries such as is sometimes experienced in continental [mainland!] Europe, relations between priests and most lay people are more distant and polite than close and warm. Some of the tolerant attitudes expressed towards priests seem rooted in an older deference to the 'man apart' and a docility more appropriate in the era of the immigrant and defensive Church. The point has been made and must be stressed again that lay compliance to clerical authority cannot be interpreted to mean normative consensus or affirmation ... A high threshold of tolerance among lay people for a wide variety of priestly styles, the passivity of the laity, and their strategies of resistance, from polite neglect to downright sabotage, and the conflicts between traditionalists and progressives among the laity themselves, all contribute to the wide variations between parishes.
>
> (ibid., pp. 143–4)

A priest interviewed in the mid-1970s, commenting on Pope Paul's encyclical *Humanae Vitae*, was quite outspoken in articulating a view of the authority of evidence, where such evidence is relevant (Hornsby-Smith, 1989, pp. 155–6). In a traditional parish in the

North Midlands in the 1980s (ibid., p. 190) there were numerous instances where the pre-Vatican priest used coercive forms of veto-power to suppress the intrusion and dissemination of views and even episcopal decisions and communications with which he disagreed. Young people were also refused communion in the hand; the selling of Catholic papers at the back of the church was suppressed and the pamphlet rack limited to a narrow range of materials; a bishop's pastoral letter was quoted only selectively and through a strong antagonistic interpretative filter; parishioners were forbidden to start prayer groups in their own homes and were allowed to discuss the preparatory documents for the National Pastoral Congress only under protest and only in a carefully planned setting under the direct and close control of the priest.

In canon law (Canon Law Society 1983) and from the perspective of the parishioner, the priest has enormous power in his parish. This is made very clear in Pope John Paul II's encyclical *Christifideles Laici* (1988), which authoritatively puts rhetoric about 'collaborative ministries' very much into context and which emphasizes that the stratification system in the Church is caste-like with no mobility between those in orders and the 'lay faithful'.

> *When necessity and expediency* [emphasis added] in the Church require it, the Pastors ... can entrust to the lay faithful certain offices and roles that are connected to their pastoral ministry but do not require the character of Orders. The Code of Canon Law, 230 No. 3 states: 'When the necessity of the Church warrants it and *when ministers are lacking,* [emphasis added] lay persons, even if they are not lectors or acolytes, can also supply for certain of their offices, namely, to exercise the ministry of the word, to preside over liturgical prayers, to confer Baptism, and to distribute Holy Communion in accord with the prescriptions of the law'. However, the exercise of such tasks *does not make Pastors of the lay faithful* [emphasis original]: in fact, a person is not a minister simply in performing a task, but through sacramental ordination.
>
> (Section 23)

In an interview in 1988, a senior priest admitted that

> there are no legal constraints on him at all ... Canon Law doesn't insist that there should be a Parish Council at all ... [A new parish priest] can in fact, destroy a parish overnight.
>
> (Hornsby-Smith, 1989, pp. 194–5)

In spite of the legal power which parish priests have, parishioners can respond with a variety of strategies for coping with a variety of

types of clerical power. These include not only alienative, calcula-
tive and moral involvement (Etzioni, 1961), but also withdrawal,
migration, avoidance or lack of involvement (possibly utilizing the
'power of the purse'), and passive conformity without normative
consent. Given the asymmetries of power between parish priests
and parishioners which are enshrined in canon law, there is always
the potential for conflict. However, it appears to be an empirical
fact that in practice conflict is rarely manifest and open. Rather it
tends to remain suppressed and latent. In the case of those with low
levels of commitment it is managed by processes of avoidance and
withdrawal. For highly committed parishioners, on the other
hand, it is controlled by processes of bargaining and negotiation
and relatively high levels of accommodation by both priests and
committed parishioners as they each learn to adapt to the expectations of the post-Vatican Church.

More recent evidence has been presented in Ryan's study *The
Catholic Parish* (1996) (also used in Barker's contribution to the
present volume). Based on interviews with around one-third of the
priests in the Birmingham archdiocese; it provides numerous examples of styles of governance assumed by these priests to be appropriate. One priest, for example, admitted:

> As a Church we are quite oppressive. We have a message to give
> and we give it. The Church tries to impose its message, not to
> offer it, even though it's a liberating message.
>
> (Ryan, 1996, p. 87)

Finally, reference can be made to the conclusions of a series of
focused interviews in the 1970s and 1980s with Catholics at every
level in the Church of England and Wales, from lay elites and
members of the former bishops' commissions to ordinary parishioners and people who attended the public events during the Pope's
visit to Britain. These researches led to the conclusion (Hornsby-
Smith, 1991, pp. 221–7) that there was an emergent plurality of
ways in which religious authority is legitimated. Our interview
data have certainly confirmed that the authority of the clerical
leadership in the Church, from the pope to the parish priest, is by
no means accepted unreservedly. Rather, contestation and conflict
are frequently found on specific matters. There is also evidence to
suggest that new forms of legitimation are emerging. The indications are that, at least to an extent, some lay people are struggling
towards more democratic forms of decision-making in what has
traditionally always been defined as being intrinsically, from its
origins, a religious community of believers with divinely instituted,

hierarchical forms of clerical authority (Canon Law Society, 1983, canons 330–572).

Recent decades have seen the emergence not only of a differentiation of religious beliefs, but also of corresponding forms of legitimation of religious authority. It might be speculated that this is an instance of a more general resistance to centralized authority. At the macro level, this has manifested itself in the struggles of local Churches against Roman centralism, as illustrated by the remark of one of the bishops around 1980 when he observed, 'it is time the local Churches took on Rome!'. Most Catholics who attended the papal events in practice made up their own minds on most matters, recognizing the Pope's teaching as offering authoritative guidelines to action. On certain issues, such as contraception, some Catholics anticipated that change would come but recognized that this would create difficulties for the religious leadership.

Catholic attitudes to clerical authority in the Church show considerable heterogeneity. On the one hand issues may be differentiated. It seems that there is a decline of, and contestation of, clerical legitimacy roughly corresponding to the differentiation between credal, non-credal, social and personal moral teachings, and the disciplinary rules and regulations of the institutional Church. There is also some evidence that progressive, middle-class Catholics are contesting older forms of clerical domination, especially at the parish level (Archer, 1986). The broad patterns of our empirical findings, therefore, lead us to the clear conclusion that there have been significant transformations in the ways in which a whole range of English Catholics have legitimated the exercise of religious authority in the Church, from the pronouncements of the Pope to the everyday realities of priest–lay relations in the parishes.

The evidence, taking Weber's typology as our starting point, showed that, like Harrison (1971), it was necessary to introduce some modifications. In particular we noted a decline of habitual forms of obedience and their replacement especially by rational-pragmatic forms of decision-making. Our findings seem to be entirely consistent with those of Cottrell (1985) in the sense that religion had salience for only a tiny minority of our ordinary Catholics, even where they were regular Mass attenders. Their outlook was also generally this-worldly and pragmatic, and this was reflected in the strength of the movement towards 'making up your own mind', especially on the issues of personal morality. There was a strong sense that popes or priests were lacking in credibility as putative authorities in these areas where the individuals themselves were alone capable of weighing all the circumstances of their everyday lives realistically and pragmatically. It is of some considerable interest and relevance that at the Synod on the Family in Rome in 1980, Cardinal Hume referred to the 'special authority in matters concerning marriage' of married couples. On the questions of the discipline concerning married priests and the doctrine concerning women priests there is evidence that many Catholics simply do not accept the arguments for the existing arrangements or consider that the 'signs of the times' have been taken on board to a sufficient extent.

It is also clear that similar views about the lack of credibility and legitimacy of the clergy as authorities on political and economic issues are widely held. Thus there were strong negative reactions to comments made by the bishops on trade unions and industrial disputes. A number of ordinary Catholics expressed a strong preference for the separation of religion and politics such as might well inhibit any strong pastoral concern with the issues of socio-economic justice.

A closer reading of our transcripts and a focusing on the question of religious authority in the Church, however, does seem to indicate a fairly diffuse and latent awareness of the distinctions between 'us', lay people, and 'them', the clergy. Insofar as there really is a democratic imperative, the likelihood is that there will be growing contestation of clerical authority in those areas where lay people feel they possess relevant knowledge and experience, while the clergy lack credibility.

Our respondents seemed in general to be opposed to absolutist moral rules. They very strongly emphasized the importance of circumstances which might alter or determine their response to any moral dilemma. This was particularly apparent in some of the comments made on abortion, where large numbers of Catholics, including regular Mass attenders, considered that the rape of an under-age girl warranted the suspension of a general prohibition of abortion. For many, perhaps the majority of the ordinary Catholics we interviewed, it was commonsensical and rational-pragmatic to take due account of the situational context in moral decision-making . Younger Catholics, in particular, are no longer motivated by the fear of hell.

It seems, therefore, that more and more Catholics are making up their own minds on more and more things and are getting on with the everyday tasks of living their lives, bringing up their families and coping with the everyday problems of child-rearing, earning a living and making ends meet, unemployment or redundancy, being good citizens, and so on, as best they can, with whatever support they can get from whatever source. It would seem that the days of substantial thought-control over all aspects of social life, powerful especially in the defensive ghettos of the fortress Church, are now well and truly over. With the removal of the threat of eternal damnation, going to church has to take its chance along with all the other claims on the discretionary time, energy and interest of English Catholics.

Social Change and the Governance of Faith

In this concluding section I attempt to summarize the main themes and to place them in context. The last half-century has seen a greater degree of social, economic, political and technological change than any comparable period in history. From a systemic perspective, adaptation of the religious sub-system was inevitable. In the case of the Roman Catholic Church, the Second Vatican Council attempted to legitimate major shifts of theological orientation while insisting on an unchanging continuity with the essential nature of the Church. Shortly after the end of the Council, Caporale interpreted modernization of the Church as 'a function of systemic interplay between membership pressure, forms of religious power and legitimate doctrinal reformulations' (1967, p. 59). Caporale suggested that whenever the Church faces potential disruption from its membership, its mechanism of control-hierarchy comes into operation. A prophetic elite within the 'hierocracy' reflects pastoral concerns and proposes innovations while official and traditional elements protest an essential continuity:

> the appeal to tradition as the ultimate criterion of legitimacy satisfies the self-definition of the Church as the continuous, unaltered Church of Christ.

> (ibid., p. 68)

As Hebblethwaite (1995), Bernstein and Politi (1996) and others have pointed out, the present papacy has encouraged the traditionalist elements in the Church. It would seem that this has led to a decline in the legitimacy accorded to the leadership in the Church and to indications of alienation ranging from quiet withdrawal and indifference to noisy rebellion and resistance. Even in Poland, the early euphoria which attended the first visit of a Slav pope changed to a more sullen politeness by the fourth visit when the Pope lectured the Poles on abortion legislation (Bernstein and Politi, 1996).

In any voluntary organization, such as the Church, some contestation of authority seems inevitable. Even more is this likely to be the case the more closely the Church approximates to a 'people of God' (*Lumen Gentium*, Abbot, 1966) or Sharing Church (*The Easter People*, Anon., 1981) organic model of the Church and the further it moves from a mechanistic, pre-Vatican model. What is important is dialogue and the search for consensus (Pottmeyer, 1996). Authority sometimes becomes legitimated by conviction in charismatic leadership (e.g. Pope John XXIII). More frequently, it seems, in the modern world it becomes legitimated by participation in decision-making where that seems relevant to those concerned. It is not that the Petrine office is rejected but that genuine horizontal and upward consultation is felt to be missing. Analogous observations can be made about the exercise of episcopal leadership at the diocesan level and priestly leadership at the parish level.

Such themes were central to the important address given by Archbishop John Quinn on the occasion of the centenary of Campion Hall, Oxford, in June 1996. It was a response to the Pope's call in his encyclical *Ut Unum Sint* (1995) on ecumenism for 'the patient and fraternal dialogue' about 'how the gift which is the papacy can become more credible and speak more effectively to the contemporary world' and 'to the Pope's invitation to rethink with him the style and manner of exercising the papal ministry "open to a new situation"'' (Quinn, 1996, p. 415). The themes he discusses include episcopal collegiality and its proper realization in the International Synods, subsidiarity, reform of the curial system, the appointments of bishops and proper consultation at the local level, and 'the tension between the political model and the ecclesial model at work in the Church'. Quinn continues in a comment which provides an appropriate conclusion to this study:

> The fundamental concern of the political model is order and therefore control. The fundamental concern of the ecclesial model is communion and therefore discernment in faith in the diversity of the gifts and works of the Spirit. The claims of discernment and the claims of order must always coexist, for one cannot be embraced and the other rejected. They must always exist in tension. But it is always wrong when the claims of discernment are all but eliminated in favour of the claims of order, thereby making control and the political model the supreme good.
>
> (*The Month*, 1996, p. 424)

Archbishop Quinn's pastoral and theological reflection is mirrored in the sociological reflections of this present study. I have endeavoured to demonstrate that both conceptually and empirically, the sociologist has much to contribute to the analysis of the exercise of authority and governance in the Church in the changing circumstance of high modernity as we approach the millennium. As Giddens (1990; 1991) points out, a key variable in social relations at the present time is that of trust. And trust in authority relationships, in the modern world, increasingly depends not only on perceived competence but also on forms of participation in dialogue and decision-making which appear to respect the dignity, competence and autonomy of those whose lives are affected. This seems to be the case both at the level of the global Church and relations between the Vatican and the local Churches, and at the local level of the diocese and the parish. Any attempt to overlook these sociological findings is likely to result in a decline of ecclesiastical legitimacy and an increase in organizational dysfunction.

References

Abbott, W. M. (ed.) (1966) *The Documents of Vatican II*, London: Geoffrey Chapman.

Anon. (1981) *Liverpool 1980: Official Report of the National Pastoral Congress*, Slough: St Paul Publications.

Archer, A. (1986) *The Two Catholic Churches: A Study in Oppression*, London: SCM.

Berger, P. L. (1973) *The Social Reality of Religion*, Harmondsworth: Penguin.

Bernstein, C. and Politi, M. (1996) *His Holiness: John Paul II and the Hidden History of Our Time*, London: Doubleday.

Burns, G. (1996) 'Studying the Political Culture of American Catholicism', *Sociology of Religion* 57(1): 37–53.

Burns, T. and Stalker, G. M. (1996) *The Management of Innovation*, London: Social Science Paperbacks.

Butler, C. (1981) *The Theology of Vatican II*, revised and enlarged edn, London: Darton, Longman and Todd.

Cadorette, C. (1989) 'Towards a Contextual Interpretation of Papal Teaching: Reflections from a Peruvian Perspective', *Social Compass* 36(3), September: 285–94.

Canon Law Society of Great Britain and Ireland (1983) *The Code of Canon Law*, London: Collins.

Caporale, R. (1967) 'The Dynamic of Hierocracy: Processes of Continuity-in-Change of the Roman Catholic System During Vatican II', *Sociological Analysis* 22(2): 59–68.

Catholic Bishops' Conference of England and Wales (1996) *The Common Good*, Manchester: Gabriel Communications.

Coleman, J. A. (1978) *The Evolution of Dutch Catholicism, 1958–1974*, London: University of California Press.

Collins, P. (1997) *Papal Power: Proposals for Change in the Earth's Third Millennium*, London: Fount.

Cottrell, M. (1985) 'Secular Beliefs in Contemporary Society', unpublished D.Phil. thesis, University of Oxford.

Dulles, A. (1976) *Models of the Church: A Critical Assessment of the Church in All Its Aspects*, Dublin: Gill and Macmillan.

Dussel, E. (1990) 'La politique vaticane en Amérique Latine: essai d'interprétation historico-sociologique' *Social Compass* 37(2), June: 207–24.

Etzioni, A. (1961) *A Comparative Analysis of Complex Organizations*, New York: Free Press.

Giddens, A. (1990) *The Consequences of Modernity*, Cambridge: Polity Press.

Giddens, A. (1991) *Modernity and Self-Identity: Self and Society in the Late Modern Age*, Cambridge: Polity Press.

Gramsci, A. (1971) *Selections from Prison Notebooks*, London: Lawrence and Wishart.

Greeley, A. M., McCready, W. C. and McCourt, K. (1976) *Catholic Schools in a Declining Church*, Kansas City: Sheed and Ward.

Habermas, J. (1976) *Legitimation Crisis*, London: Heinemann.

Hammond, P. E., Salinas, L. and Sloan, D. (1978) 'Types of Clergy Authority: Their Measurement, Location, and Effects', *Journal for the Scientific Study of Religion* 17, September: 241–53.

Harrison, P. M. (1960) 'Weber's Categories of Authority and Voluntary Associations', *American Sociological Review* 25 (April) 232–7.

Harrison, P. M. (1971) *Authority and Power in the Free Church Tradition: A Study of the American Baptist Convention*, London: Feffer and Simons.

Hebblethwaite, M. (1994) 'An Unwelcome Letter from Pope Canute', *Guardian*, 18 June.

Hebblethwaite, P. (1995) *Pope John Paul II and the Church*, Kansas City: Sheed & Ward.

Hornsby-Smith, M. P. (1987) *Roman Catholics in England: Studies in Social Structure Since the Second World War*, Cambridge: Cambridge University Press.

Hornsby-Smith, M. P. (1989) *The Changing Parish: A Study of Parishes, Priests and Parishioners After Vatican II*, London: Routledge.

Hornsby-Smith, M. P. (1991) *Roman Catholic Beliefs in England: Customary Catholicism and Transformations of Religious Authority*, Cambridge: Cambridge University Press.

Hornsby-Smith, M. P. (1996) 'Justice and Peace: Theory and Practice', *The Month* 29(1), January: 3–8.

Hornsby-Smith, M. P., Fulton, J. and Norris, M. (1995) *The Politics of Spirituality: A Study of a Renewal Process in an English Diocese*, Oxford: Clarendon Press.

Houtart, F. (1968) 'Critical Decisions and Institutional Tensions in a Religious Institution: The Case of Vatican II', *Review of Religious Research* 9(3): 131–46.

Houtart, F. (1969) 'Conflicts of Authority in the Roman Catholic Church', *Social Compass* 16(3): 309–25.

Houtart, F. (1989) 'Jean-Paul II à Managua: l'échec de la reconquête d'une espace social hégémonique', *Social Compass* 36(3), September: 327–36.

Kaiser, R. B. (1987) *The Encyclical That Never Was: The Story of the Commission on Population, Family and Birth, 1964–66*, London: Sheed and Ward.

Lukes, S. (1974) *Power: A Radical View*, London: Macmillan.

McGrandle, P. and Jenkins, J. (1996) 'Laity Protest: The Bishops Ignored Us', *Catholic Herald*, 15 November: 1.

Pottmeyer, H. (1996) 'The Reform of the Papacy' *The Tablet*, 14 September: 1188, 1190.

Quinn, J. R. (1996) 'The Claims of the Primacy and the Costly Call to Unity', *Briefing* 26(8), 15 August: 18–29 (also in *The Month* 29(11), November: 414–25).

Ryan, D. (1996) *The Catholic Parish: Institutional Discipline, Tribal Identity and Religious Development in the English Church*, London: Sheed and Ward.

Satow, R. L. (1975) 'Value-Rational Authority and Professional Organizations: Weber's Missing Type', *Administrative Science Quarterly*, 20: 526–31.

Sewell, W. H. (1985) 'Ideologies and Social Revolutions: Reflections on the French Case', *Journal of Modern History* 57: 86–96.

Sieghart, W. H. (1989) 'Christianity and Human Rights', *The Month* 22(2), February: 46–53.

Vaillancourt, J.-G. (1980) *Papal Power: A Study of Vatican Control Over Lay Catholic Elites*, London: University of California Press.

Weber, M. (1964) *The Theory of Social and Economic Organisation*, edited with an introduction by Talcott Parsons, London: Collier-Macmillan.

Weber, M. (1968) *Economy and Society: An Outline of Interpretive Sociology*, vol. 1, New York: Bedminster Press.

Willer, D. E. (1967) 'Max Weber's Missing Authority Type', *Sociological Inquiry* 37, Spring: 231–9.

Winter, M. M. (1973) *Mission or Maintenance: A Study in New Pastoral Structures*, London: Darton, Longman and Todd.

Zulehner, P. (1996) 'Austria's Naïve Reformers', *The Tablet*, 23 November: 1534–5.

Chapter Three

AUTHORITY AND THE CHURCHES

Kenneth Wilson

> Kenneth Wilson was educated at Cambridge and Bristol Universities.
> He was ordained as a Methodist minister in 1966. After chaplaincies in
> London University and Kingswood School, Bath, he taught ethics and
> philosophical theology at Wesley College and the University of Bristol,
> before in 1981 becoming Principal of Westminster College, Oxford. He
> is currently the Director of Research at The Queen's Foundation for
> Ecumenical Theological Education, Birmingham.

Introduction

All organizations in the twentieth century have shared common
problems regarding authority. In this respect the churches are in
no way to be distinguished. Indeed, in the first section of this
chapter, I shall argue that in many ways the churches have distinct
advantages in addressing the matter given the availability of the
theological traditions and theological language.

The Question of Authority

During the twentieth century we have experienced a shift from a
conservative willingness to accept traditional authorities, through
a period of apparently individualistic free-for-all to a resurgence of
a neo-conservatism. The single most significant factor has been
communication. There is nowhere to hide. No matter what the information, there is now no power in the world which can secure absolute and complete control over its distribution either in respect of
the speed or the range.

All forms of communication have to be included within this
judgement. We all have the opportunity to travel and to see for
ourselves, if we wish. Furthermore it is not simply that we can
physically move ourselves around the world and extend our own

personal experience; the technology, its speed, clarity and definition, support the word with pictures. This powerfully influences the
nature of the information available, and our understanding of the
context in which we work to form our opinions and make our judgements. Moreover we shall soon have the power to determine the information that is available to us, as the digital revolution begins to
make its full impact in the first years of the new century. There can
be no doubt that the changes in technology which will impact upon
the presentation, distribution and management of information will
have a potentially dramatic effect on our sense of personhood, of
society, and on the means by which we decide how to act in relation
to one another.

   This is hardly an original observation, but it is all too easily
ignored when there is discussion about authority. Actually what we
face today is a regular if not a constant feature of history. Ideas
depend upon communication for their impact. Moreover it is not
merely that new ideas and forms become more easily available;
perhaps even more importantly the community of interest involved
in active and critical debate is widened. Claims to authority,
whether implicit or explicit, become subject to public analysis and,
if found wanting, slip from public view. An authority which is not
discussed is no authority at all.

   The second powerful influence which has brought authority into
question is the politics of the twentieth century. Stalin, Hitler, Mao
Tse-Tung, Pol-Pot, for example, have all pretended to an authority
which, while effective for a time, led to nothing but wars and disaster for the human race. There have also been those who have
claimed religious authority, and gained it over a group of followers,
in for example the Jones debacle, or the Waco case; these have only
served to emphasize in the public mind the importance of a proper
suspicion of even religious authority. All this is consistent with a
natural human desire for leadership, for a sense of direction and
purpose, or with the willingness of individuals to claim authority
for themselves.

   The changes brought about by communication make us aware of
the huge range of conflicting ideas, systems, religions, aspirants to
power, etc., competing for our interest and support, and make us
aware of how vital it is that we take responsibility for the authorities
we accept. We know that the traditional authorities of family,
church, trade union, employer or nation, no longer have unques-
tioning allegiance. But then to what do we give authority? Suspicion
of individuals and organizations is so deep-rooted that many have
thought to find something more apparently objective and testable.

For a brief time some thought they had found just such an authority in science and its results. But while there are still those who believe that this is the only possible place to go, the majority have lost confidence, even if they ever had it, because of the profound differences of opinion among scientists, and the sometimes awful consequences of the applications of science.

These considerations highlight the key question to which answer has to be given. What authority should we accept if we as human beings are to express our true natures? On what grounds do we make the choice of choices? We shall be made as persons by the authority we accept. The Christian churches believe that they are authorized by God to witness to his authority. Given all the pressures and suspicions under which any authority operates today, how should a church conduct its affairs in order to deserve the confidence of its members, and the trust of society at large?

Towards Theological Work

Distinctions which are of the first importance are too often neglected.

Let us consider, for example, authoritarianism as opposed to authoritativeness. Authoritarianism characterizes those persons and organizations whose concern is with power and who see no need to offer justification or reason for any decisions or actions. On the other hand, authoritativeness is the quality of authority enjoyed by those organizations and persons who allow their judgements and decisions to be tested in experience. Only the latter provides the possibility of morally legitimated authority. The former may have power in the sense that its authority is acted upon, but since it is instrumental and impersonal, its authority is not moral.

In considering the nature of authority within the churches, and the appropriate exercise of that authority, one is concerned with a moral question. Authoritativeness is the focus of our interest not authoritarianism. But in the case of authority in the churches, there are fundamental theological claims of which account must also be taken. In talking of the personal as applied to God, one is using it of the being whose nature defines what it is for human being to be called personal being. Therefore, if we presume a character of the personal for the relationship between human beings and look for it even in the conduct of political organizations, all the more will it inform our understanding of the relationship between God and the world.

The Church might be thought of as that body of people brought into existence by God which has willingly responded to God's word, and accepted his grace: it is therefore necessary that the Church's behaviour in the world should be characterized by the same Spirit, and be expressed with the same grace. The authority with which the Church seeks to act internally and in relation to the world must graciously express, to the extent that it is possible, the relationship which she believes God to have with her. But that is not all. The structure in which the Church expresses her understanding of authority at any one time will be influenced by current perceptions, knowledge and skills. The understanding of God, of the way in which he exercises his authority, and therefore of the way in which the Church should structure herself in order to bear witness to the truth she has been given, will therefore have to be worked at all the time if it is to be effective. This is not to say that past understandings will be wrong, or that in order to 'make progress' everything connected with their previous implementation must be rejected. It is rather to underscore the fact that any relationship if it is to remain alive and well must be worked at, and that such work will require serious attention, and effort, and entail some risk. But in this as in other matters theological questions have much in common with other dimensions of human experience.

In creating the world, God is choosing to make himself known. That involves a decision on the part of God which is an expression of his triune nature. He has committed himself to his world by making himself available to it. In responding, as the Church, to the gracious love of God, we engage with him in a conversation which will lead to that eternal understanding which we are promised will enable us to understand even as we are understood. Of course, all our questions about the world imply in principle questions about our relationship with the world as well, and therefore questions about our own natures and our relationship with God. So in enquiring about the world we are potentially learning about ourselves, about God and about our relationship with him. God in creating has precisely opened himself to that process of interrogation and enquiry by which two persons may grow through knowledge and experience of one another to a deeper love and involvement. The risk of puzzlement and the insecurity which goes with it are essential prerequisites for this possibility. Only thus does God retain for himself the opportunity to be authoritative, and remove from himself any danger that he may become authoritarian. As a matter of fact, however, in this relationship as in others, it is the human being not the divine who is unwilling to take the risk of the possibility of knowledge (especially self-knowledge), and who seeks therefore to domesticate God in the secure determinacy of a theological system and a managed church structure. It is humankind which is inclined to fashion God after God's own image and in so doing make God into an authoritarian God – an idol. Paradoxical as it may seem, such a reduced God is powerless and devoid of any authority, because there can be no personal relationship with an idol and no moral quality to it.

These theological reflections constitute the basis of my claim that although the churches experience no isolation from the pressures which face all other authorities in the contemporary world, they have good theological reasons for accepting the present situation as normal for all human beings curious about the world and their role in it – especially for people of faith. Hence we should not be put off or upset by our present predicament, but regard it as the God-given opportunity of our continued growth in faith.

The truth of the matter is that we are not fighting against impossible odds, but learning again now to do what as churches, and as the Church, we had no right to consider we could ever give up doing.

The Experiences of the Churches

History is a dimension of all matters to do with ideas and their development. In a world of competing philosophies and theologies where argument about revelation seemed to be a matter of life and death in the day-to-day business of living, it was of the greatest importance both to know who your friends were and what to think. All the more was this the case for Christians when they were a minority in an alien world. Structures and organization had therefore to guarantee the tradition, and to be secure. The concerns of the early Church were shaped by these two factors. Of course the Fathers were also concerned *per se* with the truth of the tradition, but we should be mistaken if we did not recognize that even that profound responsibility was shaped by the historical environment in which they found themselves.

The Orthodox tradition was shaped by a theological concern. However, the context in which it had to work out how to behave, and in what way it should be structured, was one which was shaped by a sense of exile and privacy. It was not so much that the Church was persecuted, as that in order to thrive it had to form itself, as it were, from the inside. Their churches were built to reflect this. Around the walls were the saints among whom the contemporary faithful celebrated the fact of the risen Christ with their priest, who presided at the Eucharist and who, with his family, was one of them.

This real celebration of Christ's risen presence with them reminded them of God as creator and judge, the all-powerful and all-loving redeemer who despite their suffering in the world was triumphantly ever-present; hence in many churches there is the Christus Pantocrator, whose feet are planted on the same earth as theirs, whose arms surround them, and whose face looks over them. The free, earnest celebration in the action of the Eucharist shapes profoundly the authority which the Orthodox Church seeks to share.

Given the primacy of this celebration, and the lack of opportunity to shape the political or moral world in which they found themselves, it is not surprising that much less energy was put into developing a moral or political theology. Their task was to survive, to celebrate God's presence and to enjoy communion with God.

The experiences of the Church of England illustrate another dimension. For reasons of state at least as much as for theological principle, the Church of England became separated from the Roman Catholic Church. Recent historical scholarship has shown, however, just how hard the Crown and the residual authorities of the Church had to work in order to establish different practices, different doctrines and different ecclesiastical organization. It appears that the message in religious and theological terms (whatever the political facts) did not communicate itself with any great rapidity to the majority of those who were of the faith in England. On the contrary, it seems, it was their view that nothing much had changed. Therefore, the question of authority in the Church, the role of Parliament in confirming that authority, and the subsequent influence of religious ideas is of great importance. The Prayer Book of Thomas Cranmer, the changes to the role of bishops as they sought to establish their power locally, the Thirty-Nine Articles, together with the militant legislation which among other things removed the monasteries, were retrospective means whereby a Church of England was created. While it is clear that the Crown challenged the authority of the Pope, and in order to do so effectively had through Parliament to legislate so that the English church could have effective jurisdiction in its own case, it is at least possible to argue that the doctrines of the Reformation were not the reason or the occasion for the severance of relations with Rome, but the rope by which the Church in England pulled itself out of the mire in which it found itself after separation. Without that opportunity the Christian life of England would have been subject merely to the forces of royal power. The question of authority for the Church of England has the special dimension caused by the origin of that Church.

The case of the Methodist Church provides another and complementary example. Given a profound sense of the ever-present
reality of God in the world, the dire need of people cast down by
sin, and the wayward behaviour of employers and government
which exacerbated the suffering of the poor, Wesley and the Methodists simply could not believe that it was God's will that the structures and pompous greed of the established church should be
allowed to stand in the way of preaching the gospel. Therefore,
John Wesley claimed, in order not to be disobedient to the vision
and vocation vouchsafed him by God, he had no alternative but to
preach wherever the need and opportunity presented themselves.

The important point to note is how often the theology follows
from the events, not vice versa. In some cases a theology is found in
the tradition; in other cases the theology will arise by dint of hard
work, beginning usually with attention to Scripture.

Scripture, Tradition, Reason and Experience

The three dimensions of the question of authority for all the mainstream churches are Scripture, tradition and reason. To this must
be added also experience of living in the world, for history as we
have seen is not merely relevant, but necessarily so if the Church is
to remain obedient to the revelation of God in Christ. It is,
however, these very three basic factors which bring the greatest disputes and controversies.

Interpretation of Scripture has been a controversial matter since
the beginning of the Christian Church. There is evidence for this in
the way in which New Testament writers choose to quote from and
imply understandings of the Old Testament scriptures.

The role of the Holy Spirit in the authoritative interpretation of
Scripture has been accepted universally by all churches. The doctrine requires not only a faithful attention to the text, and a love of
both fellow Christians and the Church, but a recognition that the
truth which the text holds is ultimately in the hands of God. There
is therefore in one sense no understanding which is more than provisional. However, provided the motives, scholarship and imagination of the interpreter(s) are set upon doing the will of God in
Christ, then the provisional nature of the interpretation is no bar to
its making a contribution to the work of salvation, any more than
the provisional role of the Church is any bar to her vital role in
redemption.

Tradition should help us here, and perhaps the question of tradition and the interpretation of Scripture is most keenly felt when it

comes to what are believed to be the implications of doctrine for moral teaching. The churches are regularly castigated by the media because they do not speak out on moral matters. The assumption seems to be that if the pusillanimous persons in positions of authority in the Church would only look back into their traditions and confirm the traditional teachings we should all be able to get on with the proper business of living. And, after all, we all know what the Christian tradition is when it comes to the family, sexual morality, manners and public decency, international relations and guerrilla movements, birth control and socialism! The trouble is that when the tradition is carefully investigated, matters are by no means as clear as the critics would like us to believe.

It has from time to time been argued that we are saved in this situation by reason. But there are basic conflicts of interpretation here too, which a perusal of Scripture and tradition readily brings to light. There are those who on the evidence of Scripture point to human sin as demonstration of the fact that all human reasoning is fallen and therefore incapable of leading us to the truth; on the other hand there are those who would claim that human reason aided by the Spirit can at least begin to understand something of the mind of Christ, and therefore help us in our pursuit of truth. It would be hard to deny that in interpreting Scripture we employ the human reason, but equally hard to support the view that human reason unaided will provide all the resources necessary to attain to the whole truth of Scripture.

Have we therefore to fall back upon personal experience as the basis of authority for Christians? Schleiermacher believed there was no alternative and that the only unassailable authority was our 'inward feeling'. One can see his point. Given that there are no objective authorities to which one can point via Scripture, tradition or reason, but that as normal persons we need authority on which to rely, where else can we go if not to 'inward feeling'? But such isolation is hardly attractive, and in any case such confidence as we might initially have is swiftly undermined in the light of experience. Reason needs to be tested, but that puts us back into the circle from which inward feeling was supposed to provide an exit.

The prevailing influence of postmodernism comes from reflection on the same problem. If all that we have to go on is the text and our response to the tradition of interpretation, what reason have we for believing that anything we come up with as an account of the text is more than the imaginings of one mind valueless for the thinking of anyone else? Of course others may find it useful, but that would be an accident, the consequence of the fecundity of their imagination, and not necessarily anything to do with truth or God. Can we rely in the Christian Church on such an authority? Hardly, because in fact it suggests that the only determining factors are those which I choose arbitrarily to accept, whereas the basis of authority in the Christian Church is not arbitrary power but the authoritativeness which comes from membership of a faith community which encourages reasoned, faithful and affectionate enquiry about God and his relationship with the world.

The Local and the Universal Church

The relationship in all traditions between the local and the universal church depends upon the point at issue; whether for example it is a matter of doctrine concerned with the core beliefs of the Church, or something on which the Church has not yet officially and formally declared its position. It also depends upon ecclesiology. A church may think of itself as a single corporate centralized body, or churches may consider themselves to be individual communities acting with universal authority in respect of a gathered community which in principle consists of its total jurisdiction, or churches may be a federation of otherwise independent communities of faith which have negotiated a union for particular purposes.

The argument as to where authority lies may be either damaging or encouraging. However, the universal and the local have to be conceived of in association, and frequently are in practice. The Church celebrates the living God, who in his creating and redeeming presence is devoted to the whole world. The Church claims to be the body of those persons which, on behalf of all people, has begun to understand and celebrate that fact. It is vital for its wellbeing both to hold authority at the centre (i.e. universally), and also to share it locally with all who in every time and place have sought to talk through the meaning of the gospel and the significance of faith. While leaders and experts are crucial for the conduct of the conversation, the development of understanding is not confined to them, but is intended to include all people who are members of the communion of faith.

On reflection I think we would have to admit that the Church was not very good at this. Certainties and clarities are much more congenial to human beings and therefore to churches than the normal path open to us which has more in common with 'muddling-through'. Conversation, which by its nature requires diligence and application of a very demanding kind, may easily be abandoned for the lazier style of definition and exclusion. And 'muddling-

through' after all sounds to many minds like indifference or compla-
cency, which it most definitely is not. 'Muddling-through' is how we
should refer to the normal careful practice of enquiry, experiment
and action with subsequent reflection, which characterizes positive
movement towards a goal which has been clearly identified, but
where the path is not unambiguously marked. It is just the sort of
process which enables learning to take place, responsibility to be accepted, which encourages the capacity to recognize good guides and
to trust them, and which suggests that if any of us has useful clues we
should share them with others and record them for future reference.
Questions are at the heart of our growth in the faith, but so is the
issue of context. The fact that all Christians are engaged in continuing conversation is not evidence of our failure to make progress, or
of our failure to be true to the faith; it is evidence that we are alive.
The Church is a local phenomenon when it acts universally, and
universal when it acts locally.

There is another significant and even larger dimension which we
ignore at our peril: the universality which we claim is the universality on behalf of all people. The responsibility of the Church is to
take part in the universal search for meaning and purpose in which
all societies and all faiths are engaged. We shall only undestand
what we are in faith believing as we engage in conversation with
the world of enquiry outside the churches; there is more to understanding the faith than will be revealed by conversation with fellow
Christians, whether that be within or across denominations.

No amount of special-pleading, or demand of attention to the ultimate importance of God on whose authority all churches ultimately rely, will be a substitute for the hard work which is implied.

The task of the Church is to act with authority – that is continually to become authoritative, and that will only be recognized by
the world at large if we have sufficient understanding to be able to
talk with humble confidence. 'Humble confidence' is the right term
because authority comes not as a result of having at last persuaded
everyone that we have the whole truth, but because we are seen to
be wanting to share the responsibility of seeking it.

The Position of Different Churches

Churches adopt different stances with regard to the question of
authority and instantiate their understanding in different governing
structures.

THE ORTHODOX CHURCH

The fundamental difference of the Orthodox from the Roman Catholic position is that the Patriarch of Constantinople is *primus inter pares*, he does not hold an office which is in principle the one in which all authority lies. The basis of the difference is theological: whereas in the Roman Catholic tradition the office of the papacy is regarded as the one to which our Lord gave the authority to act in his name, the Orthodox Church regards the authority of Christ as having been given to his Church. It is therefore the ecumenical councils which have superior authority, and the patriarch is their servant. It is to this distinction that all the differences in the exercise of authority and the tradition of governance should be traced which do not stem from the exigencies of political, historical, moral and personal experience as Orthodoxy has striven to maintain and express its faith in its life.

Presidency of the Eucharist is the foundation of the priest's authority, and his moral integrity the basis of the authoritativeness with which he speaks.

For the world, however, the authority of the Church does not depend upon its ability to exercise power, but upon the moral integrity of its 'management' and the behaviour of its clergy. In this respect, for example, the relationship of the Greek Orthodox Church with the Greek state in the 1960s and 1970s with the direct intervention of the state in church affairs, was a serious setback. And the behaviour of the Serbian Orthodox Church in the wars which followed the break-up of Yugoslavia was equally prejudicial to its authority.

THE ANGLICAN COMMUNION

Authority and the Anglican community do not from a superficial perspective seem to mix. There are many reasons for this. First, the occasion which led to the establishment of the church in the sixteenth century was not a matter of doctrine but of practice. However, early measures to bring coherence to the new church required that a stance be taken with regard to the current theological debates of the time. Second, the ecclesiastical structure which was put in place had to acknowledge the compromise which lay at the heart of doctrinal definition and governance, a compromise which persists to this day, and in which the Anglican Communion has indeed sought to take pride and for which it is inclined to claim theological justification. Many Anglicans, however, made uncomfortable by developments within Anglicanism, have over the years left

Anglicanism to join other denominations. One thinks most recently of Bishop Graham Leonard. He was opposed to the ordination of women, but his reason for becoming a Roman Catholic was that he did not recognize that the Church of England had the authority unilaterally to choose to ordain women.

Third, the fact that the legal framework within which the Church of England worked as the established church of England, persuaded it to embrace the myth that all persons who were citizens were in principle both members of the Anglican Church and Christians, led it to assume responsibilities for which it could not be ultimately accountable.

The consequence has been a sense of crisis from time to time among Anglicans about exactly where they stood, and what were the processes by which they were entitled to change their doctrine, forms of worship or organization. In fact even where issues are apparently clear, as in the case of the liturgy and forms of worship, the controversy that has followed decision, whether parliamentary or synodical, has often led to internal dispute which ecclesiastical authority has been powerless to stem.

The accident of empire has made the Church of England incommensurate with the Anglican Communion. The nomenclature of the various structures by which the Anglican Communion currently manages itself is instructive. There is the Anglican Consultative Council, at which representatives of worldwide Anglicanism meet to debate, discuss and encourage one another. There is the Lambeth Conference, which has met every ten years since 1868 and which all bishops attend. The Archbishop of Canterbury presides, but neither he nor the Conference has any statutory authority. A Primate's Meeting takes place between meetings of the Lambeth Conference but has no more authority than the primary body. The synods of the various provinces meet once or twice per year and do, for their respective provinces, have an authority which is binding on the constituent dioceses.

In addition to the consultation processes, and the decision-making procedures of the synods, Anglican tradition accepts the historical, theological, and practical significance of the bishop's personal responsibility. It is worth noting that while the synods of the Church of England authorized the ordination of women, they did not make any changes with regard to the consecration of bishops. There can, therefore, be no women bishops. This is likely to be matter for the conversations between the Methodist Church and the Church of England: Methodists will want to know why, if it is possible to ordain women, it is not possible to consecrate women as bishops.

A bishop increasingly exercises discipline over the clergy in his diocese. Traditionally his power had been limited by the parson's freehold, but when that was ended by Parliament the bishop gained the power not only to appoint clergy but to remove them.

The Anglican Church, like other Christian churches of the main stream, accepts the authority of Scripture, tradition, reason and experience. This church does not, however, have a structure of governance which allows it to use these authorities so as to define in all particulars what its position actually is. In many ways, especially since it is the established church, it is therefore an easy target for those who wish to find scapegoats for the moral turpitude of our times, or for those Christians who are very clear about more things (especially regarding sexual morality) than the Church is. If there is unclarity in the authorities, of course, the wise position is to recognize that. The generous understanding of the responsibilities of every Christian, which attributes to each a common accountability, underlines the Anglican Church's acceptance of authoritativeness rather than authoritarianism as the character of the authority which it enjoys. There is no ultimate authority within the Church or England or the wider Anglican Communion which can remove from the individual Anglican (or of course in principle any Christian) the responsibility to choose how to behave. This is a strength provided there is a will to remain in one united conversation. Hence the Church of England has a profound fear of schism. The uncomfortable consequences are there for all to see. It is tempting to say that they always will be if the Church is doing its job.

It is confusing, for example, that one province of the Anglican Communion can approve what another disapproves. Thus the decision of the English synods to ordain women in 1993 did not determine the outcome for the disestablished church in Wales, whose synod did not agree until 1996.

Such cases testify not only to the Anglican Communion's breadth, but to its willingness to accept the practical consequences of its theological position. Its lack of a defined position on many matters, combined with its open approach to decision-making, conspire at this present time to deprive it of authority in the minds of many of its members and of the nation. Paradoxically, it may be this very openness which will make it aware of the prompting of the spirit and the mind of Christ. The concept of the Church implicit here is a community of the faithful *in via*, focused on Christ its head, anxious to do his will, but unwilling to foreclose on matters finally, for to do so

would be to translate the present *consensus fidelium* by transcendental
deduction into uncriticizable and therefore unintelligible statements. Such rigid statements would stultify the doctrine of creation,
and by denying the human creature any part with God in creating,
preclude the possibility of redemption and the ultimate knowledge
of God which it is our faith that we are promised.

Whereas one can have a Baptist church, there is no such thing as 'the
Baptist Church'. Behind this statement there lie almost all the dimensions of the matter of authority as it affects the Baptist, because
it is necessarily with the individual believer that we have to begin.
The question for the Baptist is, as a free-thinking spirit, how he or
she is to understand which is the truth of God and what is his
purpose. What is more, that purpose is first and foremost seen as his
purpose for the individual believer. It was this question which
faced the first Baptists in the early seventeenth century as they
wrestled with the fact that the critical doctrine of Believers'
Baptism threatened to separate them from the vast majority of
other Christians, and the established church in particular.

The first Baptists held it to be obvious that literal Scripture attested to the doctrine of Believers' Baptism. Therefore they believed
that they had no option but to separate themselves and to meet
with like-minded believers in churches which they established and
to which the members themselves called persons to be pastors. The
pastors were given the respect due to the office if they were faithful
to Scripture and tradition, as Baptists interpreted them, but all
members had a share in discerning the Lord's will for the congregation and there could be no question of the pastor assuming all
power. If such a situation was to arise, that would be as much the
fault of the congregation for failing to fulfil their responsibilities as
it would be that of the pastor for failing to understand the role. In
the event that a member of the congregation transgressed the rules
to which membership committed them, the deacons (elected lay
leaders of the local church) could by vote exclude them. In practice
today members exclude themselves by failing to attend, and are excluded by default as a result of a resolution of the deacons' meeting.

The many Baptist churches are subject to no ecclesiastical
authority beyond that of their own individual constitution; that is
not a licence to believe and do anything they choose since every
Baptist church accepts Scripture, tradition and experience as
authoritative, and the guidance of the Spirit so sought to be defini-

tive. Reason is also accepted, though with less confidence and with more possibility of conflict than in some other traditions, such as the Anglican. The reason for this is the belief in sin, which as far as the Baptist is concerned undermines the likelihood that reason is capable of revealing the will of God. However, since the world in all its dimensions, including the powers of the state, the work of scientists and the creative genius of technicians, derives what authority it has from God, it is important to take their evidence into account as well. There is no legitimate escape for the individual Baptist; he or she is personally responsible for the authority to which he or she gives allegiance; he or she is answerable to God ultimately for that choice.

It is this irremediable condition which leads some Baptists, and therefore some Baptist churches, to refuse to give any authority to the Baptist Union, or at least to be very suspicious of it even when they choose to be a part of it. The Baptist Union is a voluntary association of Baptist churches, membership of which presumes certain doctrinal conditions, but its primary purpose is to make resources available for missionary work (that is to pay for ministers, buildings or other services). This practical basis for association hardly constitutes an ecclesiology, and provides no theological basis for a super-church authority.

The special importance of the Baptist churches lies in their diversity, their large membership and their relative coherence; it is their understanding of the nature of authority in the Church, and their trust in the Spirit, which led to them being of such influence in Central Europe during the period of the Russian Empire. They were able to act with a local authority which presumed a universal reference, and with a certainty which kept at bay the secular influence of atheistic Marxism.

In one sense the question of authority for a Baptist church is remarkably uncomplicated. It lies with the individual, and that is all there is to it. There is no court beyond that of the local congregation, short of God himself.

THE METHODIST CHURCH

Methodism was born out of a boundary crisis. John Wesley was an eighteenth-century rational enthusiast for God as he found him to be revealed in Jesus, and the Bible, and his Church. John Wesley was an ordained Anglican priest who, when denied by some bishops the opportunity to preach in their dioceses, found that he was unable any longer to accept their authority. Since, as he saw it, they no longer witnessed to the universality of God's grace, to the possibility of holiness and perfection for all, they were not fulfilling their roles as guardians of the Faith and preachers of the gospel.

In stepping outside the jurisdiction of the Church, Wesley was putting himself at risk, he believed, in order not to reject the love of God which for him was the ultimate authority. However, it would be a mistake to conclude that Wesley himself or the subsequent Methodist societies, churches, or the present Methodist Church of the United Kingdom did not have a clear decision-making structure. In many ways it could appear to the observer that of all the Free Churches its governance was the most clearly defined. The precision comes partly from the ambiguity within Methodism concerning understanding whether it is a church or a society within the Church. Wesley chose to obey God rather than bishops, but he was not following a predetermined programme to create an independent body, The Methodist Church. On the contrary it could be argued that only when the Church of England saw him to be schismatic, and he realized that for the time being at least he had to take seriously the care of those whom God had converted under his preaching, did he take into the Methodist community those marks of the Church which he regarded as essential: ordination and sacramental celebration. He regarded himself as entirely justified in doing so. Christian believers need pastors and sacraments; all the evidence he had was that God had called him to preach the gospel since all around him there were growing numbers of faithful souls who, having been converted by him, were meeting together to worship God and to encourage one another in the faith. It was not his will that they should meet apart from the faithful of the Church of England, but when they were excluded he felt the time had come to provide for them.

The two basic authorities within the Methodist Church are the annual Conference (consisting of persons, lay and ordained) and the circuit superintendent minister whose role is effectively to be compared with that of the bishop. It is the Church in Conference which votes to ordain a person who has been nominated by a local church, approved by a district synod and educated by the church. The members of the Conference, which is sovereign in all matters, are elected by the district synods. Discipline over ministers is reserved to a ministerial session of the Conference. Matters of doctrine, order or organization may begin discussion in the ministerial session but will be further subjected to scrutiny by the full Conference. In fact most important legislation is provisional. When first voted upon by the Conference in full session the decision is only to send it down to district synods and circuit meetings for their opinions; it returns the following year for ratification or modification in the light of the opinions expressed.

Recently there has been much concern within the church that decisions took too long, that resources were wasted on bureaucracy which should be devoted to mission, and that organization was too diffuse to give practical effect to the primary purposes of the church. This has resulted in the establishment of a Methodist Council with executive power to look after affairs between Conferences. None of this, in principle, threatens the paramount position of Conference or the role of the superintendent minister in a circuit; it remains to be seen whether the new structure offers that degree of sensitivity to the practicalities of a local situation and the external environment on which in the long run all effective authority depends. Without understanding and sympathy, no 'authority' will be authoritative. Top-down implies bottom-up when it comes to real authority; never more so than when it comes to the Methodist tradition.

The international position of the Methodist Church is rather different and needs briefly to be alluded to. The Methodist Church in the United Kingdom continues to decline; it therefore suffers from a renewed sense of being on the margins, an experience exacerbated by the media's virtually exclusive attention to the established church and the Roman Catholic Church. In America too, along with the other mainstream churches, the United Methodist Church is suffering from a credibility gap, especially when it comes to the younger generation. However, globally, in South America, Africa and particularly the Pacific rim, there is a different story. This phenomenon has led to greater attention being given to the International Council of Methodism. The membership includes all Methodist Churches worldwide, but it has absolutely no authority other than that which comes from the quality of the work it does and the publications it promotes.

THE UNITED REFORMED CHURCH

The United Reformed Church is, as its name implies, a united church in the Reformed tradition. It came about as a result of long negotiations between the Presbyterian and Congregational Churches in the United Kingdom. Though not all of the individual congregations in either denomination agreed to the merger, the central bodies of each church accepted that they represented a sufficiently large majority for the decision to be taken to proceed. The decision raises the question of the extent to which the resulting church can constitutionally and doctrinally be said to involve a compromise. The question is important because there have been no other cases where successful unions have taken place in the United Kingdom: it remains to be seen whether now that a decision has been taken by the Methodist and Anglican Churches to talk about closer relations, they can do so in such a way as to keep open the possibility of uniting.

The Scheme of Union makes clear the position of the United Reformed Church with regard to the source and exercise of authority. The primary authority is Scripture, which is interpreted in and by the Church under the guidance of the Holy Spirit. The key perspective is, however, in a sense future; the Church is anxious that it does not close itself off to the continued prompting of the Spirit, and therefore specifically 'affirms its right to make such new declarations of faith and for such purposes as may from time to time be required by obedience to the same Spirit'. The various questions that arise all seem to concern a church which is trying to come to a common mind about the meaning of Scripture and finding that at the moment it is not possible to do so. The Church as a whole is involved because of the acceptance of the principle of corporate responsibility. The mind of the Church is sought through a public process of consultation involving a general assembly, provincial synods, district meetings, church meetings and meetings of elders (locally elected lay leaders): all may expect to be led by the Holy Spirit and guided by Scripture. However, corporate responsibility involves a sense of history and tradition, and partnership with other Christians in ecumenical dialogue from which it is expected that the URC will learn also of the leading of the Holy Spirit. It is of great interest that the current position differs considerably from the previous position of Congregationalism. In Congregationalism it was assumed that the church meeting was the sole context where the guidance of the Holy Spirit should be sought. The ecumenical movement, insofar as it has brought together Presbyterianism and Congregationalism, has done so in such a way as to enlarge their perspective of the context in which the guidance of the Holy Spirit may be sought and therefore the range of reference from which it is appropriate to draw in order to find the Christian authority which is authoritative. It could therefore be said that Congregationalism had in one sense compromised, but only if one ignored the open perspective which the tradition had always embraced with regard to the leading of the Spirit, and its determination to accept the authority of Christ.

Sectarian Authority

The title of this section virtually declares the perspective of authority which those Christian communities included will assume. They
do not accept the generally authoritative status of the four perspectives, Scripture, tradition, experience and reason. In reverse order,
they are inclined to reject reason, to deny the roles of experience
and tradition, and to give all authority to Scripture, and the power
of the Spirit which objectively and of himself confirms the truth of
what is revealed to the mind of the faithful individual, and the community. It is precisely because in these communities there can be
no ambiguity, it is claimed, in the definition of what is believed and
how it is interpreted, that they are successful and have authority.
Indeed it is their very authoritarianism which justifies them in the
eyes of their members. Such a position, while intelligible in a
period such as our own, is wrong both practically and theologically,
because it makes no room for faith and therefore prevents what it
claims to promote – the emergence of a personal relationship
between God and the believer.

Such beliefs have been common throughout Christian history and
the conflicts associated with them regular and often disturbing.
There is always the temptation for mainstream traditions to envy
their 'easy' position and to wish to emulate them. The temptation
has never been greater than the present. After all, we are pressed
by the secular world to say where we stand (particularly) on moral
issues, and by atheistic non-believers to confirm that we do indeed
believe the naively literal statements of doctrine which they claim
real believers must accept. Furthermore, those who are concerned
to 'manage' the churches, and to whom responsibility has been
given under God for their well-being, are naturally inclined to
want to rein things in. Nothing could be more tempting when
members of our own communities are themselves seduced into accepting new sectarian authorities because they believe they have
been let down by the lack of authority of the church of their birth.
All such temptations have to be resisted if we are to be true to the
understanding of authority assumed in this chapter, and which I
believe underlies the approach to which all the churches aspire, as
they seek by their life and witness to be faithful to the God whose
presence they celebrate in worship.

Conclusion

The question of authority will be one with which human society
engages universally and always. Philosophical and scientific

enquiry, technical development especially in the field of communications, questions about the nature of consciousness, the legitimacy of political and economic power as it is exercised nationally, regionally and internationally, amongst many others, will all continue to complicate the discussion of authority.

It is impossible to think that the churches could be excused their share of the work. Indeed, it has been my contention that by engaging in the debate about authority in the Church, and the way in which it should best be exercised so as to witness to the God in whom they believe, the churches have the opportunity to contribute in a major way to human maturity.

I therefore presume that theology will be the primary context of enquiry about the nature of authority in the Church. Such an enquiry will continue to take greater note of the results of biblical scholarship, of historical study, of the impact of experience on the life and practice of Christian communities. However, the holistic nature of our understanding of our experience, and the changes in the way we conceive of ourselves in the light of increasing and changing knowledge of ourselves and the world in which we are set, also have implications for the way in which we conceive of the reality that is God, Father, Son and Holy Spirit. And this implies that we will have to give special attention to the role of reason, how it is to be developed, educated and expressed.

In connection with this we have to look all over again at the question of natural theology: I speak from within a Methodist tradition, of course, which has in fact made assumptions about the possibility of natural theology while at the same time failing to encourage its study. In other Protestant traditions it has been argued to be impossible given the sinful nature of human being. Yet without a possibility of a role for reason in the pursuit of God and the clarification of faith in him, how can we be held responsible for the decision to put our trust in God and make him authoritative for us? And if we are not capable of such responsible judgements, then in what sense are we human and made in the image of God?

The structure of church government will need continually to be kept under review so that it encourages Christian believing that is mature and responsible. St Paul's use of the word *akouō* is frequently translated 'obey'; however, the term also embraces importantly the notion of 'understanding'. An authority which is not understood is one which cannot have been wholly accepted. Perhaps we are approaching a period of history for the churches when in partnership with one another, we can set out to bring into the fellowship of the Holy Spirit all our understandings, theories, practices, developments, questions and problems, so as to bring a new natural theology and a new systematics into fruitful existence which will command our common allegiance. No imposed authority will be a substitute for such a quest. And quest I call it, because we would fool ourselves and betray the revelation which we have received, if we thought that any systematization which we could construct would be more than a temporary intellectual shelter on our way to the peak of the mountain. The most authoritative statement we can make is that there is a peak; we should take comfort in that and say it more clearly and with conviction.

Chapter Four

THE LESSON OF THE VOLUNTARY SECTOR: HAS THE CHURCH SOMETHING TO LEARN?

Terry Connor and Sarah Lindsell

Terence Connor read Spanish and Latin-American studies before pursuing a career in social work. After postgraduate study at the University of Kent and the London School of Economics and appointments in social services departments in London he became Director of the Catholic Children's Society in 1982. He has been Vice-Chair of the National Council of Voluntary Child Care Organisations and is currently Chair of British Agencies for Adoption and Fostering.

Sarah Lindsell is the Chief Executive of Guildford Action for Community Care, a charity concerned with the needs of people with low incomes. After studying at University College Cardiff and the London School of Economics, Sarah has worked in the voluntary sector for 15 years, in the UK and overseas in a range of countries including Indonesia and the United States, in both paid and voluntary capacities. She is a trustee of several charities and has published several books, most recently one on family centres. An active Catholic at parish and diocesan level, Sarah is married with a young child.

Introduction

Since dioceses and parishes are subject to the Charity Commission it is essential to analyse them from the perspective of charitable activity. In this chapter (originally written in response to the article 'Leadership in a Voluntary Movement' by Jan Kerkhofs (in Kerkhofs, 1995), which considers the Church as having many of the characteristics of the secular voluntary movement), we are seeking to provoke discussion and to justify further investigation of the theory that the Church should be seen as a voluntary organization and a key player in the world of voluntary activity.

Why Look at the Church as a Voluntary Organization?

Authority and governance present critical challenges for the Catholic Church today. Authority in the Church has been described as 'the issue behind the issues' and papal authority exercised by the Vatican has increasingly been viewed by many Catholics as restrictive and stultifying. Indeed papal pronouncements such as *Humanae Vitae* have failed to find an echo with the majority and it has been suggested that authoritarian control over the people of God is a denial of the pastoral nature of Jesus' command to Peter. 'Feed my sheep' (John 21.17). In voluntary organizations the parameters for the exercise of authority and governance are determined by the constitution and mission statement. The Catholic Church, however, has no formal constitution. Centralized governance, as currently exercised, falls short of the conciliar vision of the Church and the structure of governance far removed from that of a voluntary organization in which trustees carry specific responsibilities. Since the Church is arguably a voluntary organization, what may be gained by a closer approximation to the relevant operative norms in terms of governance and authority? The governing bodies of voluntary organizations carry ultimate authority and are independent of the executive. Policy is approved and evaluated by trustees and implemented by paid staff. In the Church the bishops are similarly involved with both governing body (trustees) and executive (paid staff).

The Church, like many voluntary organizations, relies on the commitment of its members. As an employer, it shares some of the characteristics of bureaucracies and also has much in common with membership associations. While Sunday Mass attendance may not be the only determinant of 'membership', an estimated 50,000 annual decrease must be a matter of concern: not least because the Church, like many voluntary agencies, combines three distinct elements: a service bureaucracy, a voluntary membership association and a pattern of informal social relations. It is 'voluntary' in the very real sense that it needs to cultivate the willing participation of those who profess to belong, but church membership is no longer guaranteed and mobility on the basis of free choice has implications for voluntary participation. The Church as an organization characterized by norms of beneficence, authority and hierarchy could find itself increasingly at variance with members, particularly young people, and may need to learn to speak the new language which 'recognises what the voluntary world has known all along – that organisations are living communities with a common purpose, made up of citizens with minds and values and rights of their own' (Handy, 1988).

Accountability is a major issue for the Church in its struggle with conflicting value systems, styles of governance and the management of its human and financial resources. Increased lay involvement and debate about the role of women in the Church raises issues of equal opportunity and empowerment which are also priorities within the voluntary sector.

A study of the Church from the perspective of a voluntary organization could be fruitful in terms of an examination of issues relating to the experience of change and the effects of the exercise of power over different groups. Specific theories developed within the voluntary sector could inform particular debates. Resource dependency theory, for example, suggests that voluntary organizations adjust in response to changes in the amount and type of resources available to them. Both the shortage of priests and decreasing income through falling Mass attendance could be influential in decisions relating to future organization. Resource dependence has been identified as a prime factor in the reorganization of voluntary organizations.

Well-publicized scandals of child abuse by paedophile priests and widespread betrayal of celibacy by clergy at all levels have eroded the moral authority of the Church. The apparent inconsistency of welcoming married Anglican clergy whilst maintaining the rule of celibacy to indigenous priests has increased confusion and contributed to the loss of organizational credibility. The way in which the Church is confronting what many consider to be an organizational crisis seems far removed from one management theorist's description of the Church in the 1950s as 'the oldest, largest and most successful organisation of the West' (Drucker, 1968). Organizational crisis and change have emerged as important challenges within the voluntary sector and there is a steadily accumulating body of research experience available which could be of assistance in understanding some of the issues now confronting the Church.

Thus issues of accountability, authority and governance are core elements in critical debate on the Church as an organization, as are problems of membership associations, equal opportunity and change.

*How Does the Church Resemble Agencies within the
Voluntary Sector?*

The Church is akin to many organizations in the voluntary sector as
regards characteristics and challenges. Churches

> share with other non profit organisations features such as a strong
> underpinning value commitment, dependence on volunteers,
> multiple constituencies and multiple goals. They also have
> shared experiences of organisational difficulties surrounding for
> example, the relationship between local and national units; the
> relationship between staff and 'lay' people; competition between
> stakeholders; and organisational growth and change.
>
> (Harris, 1995, p. 296)

Tensions within voluntary agencies apply equally to the Church:
e.g. in the fields of decision-making; equal opportunities; role confusion between staff and volunteers; relationships between HQ
and the locality; funding; organizational change; accountability;
evaluation and monitoring.

By recognizing the Church as a major institution within our
society we are obliged to reflect on its position within the agencies
meeting social need. Up to the present churches and congregations
have been viewed in isolation, although they have frequently been
key contributors in terms of welfare provision. The provision of
care may be defined in terms of: the *personal*, in which problems are
resolved and needs met individually without a contractual arrange-
ment; the *voluntary*, where groups of people draw a boundary
around themselves and others to meet some need; and finally the *bureaucratic*, which consists of the private and statutory sectors and
also involves the hierarchical organization of paid staff. The voluntary sector thus comprises the voluntary world and the ambiguous
zones to which it lies closest.

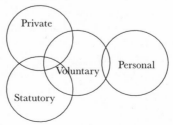

The 'voluntary' world is diverse, heterogeneous, complex, interrelated and changeable. Not only is it intricate but an intense
source of contention snd discrepancy for those trying to ascertain

or define core characteristics. However, despite the many definitions the Church will sit comfortably within each interpretation. Indeed, Horton-Smith categorizes the Church into various typologies and firmly claims it to be part of the non-profit sector (Horton-Smith et al., 1980). Similarly, the Church is placed solidly within Billis's definition in which the voluntary sector is seen as a collection of organizations that are

(a) formal or institutionalized to some extent;
(b) private, i.e. institutionally separate from government;
(c) non-profit distributing, i.e. not returning profits generated to their owners;
(d) self-governing, i.e. equipped to control their own activities; and
(e) voluntary, i.e. involving some meaningful degree of voluntary participation.

Recent studies have demonstrated the Church to be at the heart of volunteer activity and it may be argued that it serves as a core provider of informal care and that it increasingly meets social need.

The Church can thus be described as a voluntary agency and also as sharing organizational characteristics and challenges with other agencies within the voluntary sector. Using a sectoral view of society, the Church is placed firmly in the non-profit sector and it could thus be beneficial to base practice upon voluntary sector theories. This could provide insight into Church organization, especially in relation to governance and authority; it would help to explain problems and challenges and could provide the Church with tools to govern, organize and manage its activities so as to complement limited organizational theory. It may however be argued that the Church possesses key features which distinguish it from the voluntary sector.

Implications and Benefits of Using Voluntary Sector Theory to Explore Organizational Issues within the Church

'The application of management to the Church arouses instinctive opposition.'

(Carr, 1985)

There are three key areas to be explored: the organizational; surrounding issues of accountability; and finally the structures of governance and authority within the Church in the light of voluntary sector theory.

ORGANIZATIONAL ISSUES

User involvement and equal opportunities

Growth in consumerism has led to changes in the internal structure and culture of many voluntary organizations. User involvement is now a key feature of voluntary organizations, many of which consider themselves 'voluntaristic' only to the extent that their intended beneficiaries are significantly involved in decisions about goals and policy. If these principles were to be applied to the organizational structure of the Church, fundamental questions would arise with regard to the role of the laity and in particular to the position of women within the Church. Issues of equal opportunity would also arise concerning qualifications with regard to specific parish tasks; the present (closed) system of allocating and transferring priests around the dioceses and, perhaps most importantly, the (closed) appointment of diocesan bishops by the Vatican. At parish level the Church and the celebration of the Eucharist are identified with the ordained ministry. Yet as Nicholas Lash has eloquently suggested:

> within the community of the Church there is a wide variety of different jobs to be done, services to be rendered, gifts of the Spirit to be deployed for the building up of the community in the knowledge, love and service of God.
>
> (1977, p. 45)

Paid staff and volunteers

Voluntary sector literature has much to offer at the interface between paid staff and volunteers. Voluntary organizations use volunteers to a greater or lesser extent as trustees, project workers or fundraisers. Their involvement generally presupposes a desire to contribute to the ideology or values of the organization. This appeal to shared values becomes problematic once the accepted ideology and shared value system begins to disintegrate. Etzioni in his classification of organizations characterized voluntary agencies as predominantly normative. Such a classification raises particular issues for the Church in which compliance is based on moral authority and the inducement to 'volunteer' results from moral identification.

The European Values Study explored volunteer participation within the context of moral and social attitudes. Core church members were over-represented in all fields of voluntary activity. However, widespread disengagement and an ageing church membership suggests that there may be problems about the replacement of today's volunteers.

The present shortage of priests means that parish life, in the sense in which it is understood to relate specifically to the clergy, is no longer restricted to those who are 'employed' or who receive direct payment for the activities in which they are engaged. The attempt to do 'more with less' in terms of human resources is common to the Church and the voluntary sector in which the demands upon voluntary organizations have increased while the number of volunteers has remained more or less static.

Voluntary sector studies suggest that particular problems arise around the recruitment, motivation and management of people for whom the link between work and pay is absent. While there is a need for professional staff and volunteers to work side by side, this can lead to problems. Kerkhofs suggests that 'larger organisations need real professionals who are sometimes attracted from outside. However, the efficiency of their skills in no way replaces the dynamic of the distinctive inspiration of the movement' (1995, p. 148). The ability or otherwise of the Church to create a climate conducive to wider participation in the governance of the organization is likely to be of major importance and hinges on whether or not it is able to see its volunteer base as something more than a tool for coping with specific tasks in a climate of financial uncertainty.

Role of the clergy

While the role of the clergy is unique to the Church and differs from that of staff working in the voluntary sector, certain aspects of the relationship between clergy and lay workers are common to many charities. Indeed, Harris states that

> problems surrounding the relationship between clergy and lay groupings might be informed by research on the relationship between professional staff and non-profit boards which suggests that the relationship is appropriately understood as contingent, interdependent and negotiable.

> (1995, p. 269)

The clergy are 'employed' to carry out a job and are thus subject to the usual legal, traditional responsibilities and accountabilities. However, they also have a curious status which carries authority separate from their 'employment' and is seen to derive ultimately from God. This ambiguity reflects on their relationship with lay leaders and parishioners. Thus, for example, Harris, in her study of the organizational features of religious congregations, demonstrated the difficulty of defining the appropriate authority relationship between a parish priest and a full-time highly educated lay pastoral worker. Others argue that there is a conflict between the priest as leader who carries importance and authority, and the priest as servant of the people. Parishioners often have competing demands and expectations of their priest, hence 'clergy are faced with a great volume and breadth of potential responsibilities and major dilemmas as they try to prioritise their work and implement their roles' (Harris, 1995, p. 263). Clergy, and in particular the parish priests, are expected to be all things to all people. As Lauer states, the priest is required 'to compete and yet to love, to be a man of God, yet equally apt in organising and administering, to be diligent in study and prayer, yet faithful in visiting, listening, planning' (1973, p. 195). If for the purposes of organizational structure, priests and deacons are considered as 'employed' staff, there is considerable merit in reflecting on the nature of experience and training required to manage what are effectively voluntary organizations, throughout the length and breadth of the country. Kerkhofs states that clergy, like practitioners in the voluntary sector, have expressed the desire for clear terms of office rather than a lifetime commitment which must be fulfilled obediently. But, 'the problem touches on a delicate question in the theological tradition, namely the permanent character of the priesthood'. Although 'in certain pastoral councils it is being asked whether pastors of around thirty could be called for a possibly limited time, and even be given ordination, including priesthood' (1995, p. 153), the Church has little or no experience of such limited-term appointments.

'Presidents, university rectors and chairs of almost all governing bodies are in principle elected for a limited period' (p. 153). Most voluntary agencies have standardized policies for recruitment, misconduct, elections and re-nominations. The main reason for this is that such policies

> offer protection against the abuse of power and against rigidity. In addition there is a concern to avoid a particular generation monopolising decision-making power for too long because of increased expectation of life ... and in order to guarantee the dynamic expectation of the movement.
>
> (p. 157)

While voluntary organizations have both benefited and suffered under long-term leadership by a single individual (founder or charismatic leader), the need for sustainability of the agency and the competing demands of the environment have shown that limited terms of office with adequate levels of training, supervision and management are essential to effective organization. The need for continuous training is highlighted by Kerkhofs, who states that 'investigations in all countries are showing that many priests are not prepared to work in teams with laity whether professionals or volunteers, above all if these are women' (p. 153). It could be further argued that both voluntary agencies and the Church have limited experience of the importance of the recruitment and selection of personnel.

Goals and purposes

Voluntary sector experience demonstrates the importance of establishing goals and agreeing the methods of achieving these. It is perhaps unsurprising that problems with clarifying goals and defining purpose are frequently found in voluntary agencies in crisis. Similar challenges have faced the Church in recent times, e.g. when traditional theological and spiritual goals conflict with the psychological and social demands of society. The reconciliation of such tensions is both time-consuming and organizationally exhausting and it has been argued that such problems of organizational maintenance conflict with religious values. In addition, the Church faces difficulties comparable to those of campaigning organizations who seek to raise awareness but find it fatiguing to be politically controversial while attempting to attract the attention of indifferent potential audiences.

HQ and locality

A frequent tension highlighted by clergy and lay people is that which exists between the parish and the diocese and between the diocese and other levels within the hierarchy. Much of this, however, can be explained in terms of 'studies of local groups and headquarters organisations in secular non profits; studies which demonstrate pulls between centralisation and decentralisation and the ways in which local units trade autonomy for resources' (Bailey, 1992; Young, 1989; Zald, 1970). The challenge facing the Church and every voluntary agency with headquarters and branches is that of how to maintain the cohesion of the institution and the utility of the central body (the Vatican) while accommodating the desires of local groups (parishes) for sufficient autonomy to allow them to respond appropriately to local need within the capacity of local resources. Autonomy is thus defined as the ability of parishes to take decisions for themselves on issues which would normally be dealt with higher up in the church hierarchy.

Some of the key problems which voluntary organizations face can also be seen in the Church. These include alienation, conflict and misunderstanding between the local and central bodies, conflict regarding goals and purposes; tension over policy-making; loyalties; the organization of funding (in terms of both distribution and the generation of income); the role of local stakeholders; accountability and responsibility. Key concepts within the voluntary sector as in the Church are those of power, control and authority, and both explanations and solutions to problems may be found within documentation relating to the voluntary sector.

Various models are used to explain relationships between the local and central body of an organization. Scott distinguished between the *autocratic* structure which is highly centralized and controlled by a hierarchy; the *totalitarian* structure in which control is exercised by means of coercion; the *democratic* agency in which participation is encouraged; and the *federalized* organization in which coordination is both hierarchical and participative and which implies a high degree of autonomy. The chosen structure is said to depend upon environment, goals and resources. Dominance and rigidity of a particular model could help to explain some of the problems of authority and control experienced by the Church in terms of the relationship between the parish and the central bodies of the Church.

Organizational change

> There is nothing more difficult to carry out, nor more doubtful of success, nor more dangerous to handle than to initiate a new order.
>
> (Machiavelli)

Change is usually feared, it disturbs the status quo, threatens vested interests and inevitably takes longer than anticipated. This is no less true for the Church than for the wider voluntary sector. All voluntary organizations are subject to planned change and to environmental change, e.g. ideological shifts, changes in professional standards and funding which are seen as either threat or opportunity. Resistance to change is likely to be strong, whether this takes the form of pockets of resistance, partial implementation, dilution or complete rejection. Lessons from the voluntary sector have shown that change is resisted for several reasons: fear of the unknown; the need for security and stability; a perceived threat to vested interests; incorrect information; lack of resources to assist the process; and an uneven balance of power. That said, the authority vested in the Church is one of the major factors inhibiting change as authority structures 'are based (and/or) justified to a considerable extent on theological principles' (Cantrell et al., 1983, cited by Harris, 1995). While the Church requires both dynamism and cohesion 'many of those in office and many faithful can see how the organisation is holding the movement in a straight jacket' (Kerkhofs, 1995, p. 160).

Like other large, traditional, bureaucratic charities, the Church has a mechanistic structure, but it operates within a world which promotes and benefits from an 'organic' structure. As a bureaucracy, the Church has no mechanism to facilitate change apart from the existence of a state of crisis. Its structure does not permit autonomy and seldom any degree of flexibility or the rapid response to local need. It is centuries old, views itself in isolation and in no way as interdependent or interrelated with other organizations alongside whom it operates. Voluntary agencies, however, have learnt not only that such a perception is ineffective but that it is organizationally damaging. Organizations must be able to respond to changes in the environment and to move on from Weber's original definition of bureaucracy.

Studies have shown that the more stable, hierarchical and established an agency, the greater the likely resistance to change. There are, however, established theories and strategies of change which have proved themselves applicable to the voluntary sector, which has a reputation for responding well to change and 'can be highly adaptive to changed circumstances and responsive to new demands' (Powell and Friedkin, 1987, p. 180). The unique religious value base of the Church formulates its own strategy for change which can result in both a powerful incentive for change and an impenetrable block (e.g. collaborative ministry and lay involvement on the one hand and on the other a belief that women should be barred from clerical office).

Once again, developing theories of structure and organizational design which are applicable to the Church could explain and offer solutions to organizational difficulties. Harris takes this further and states that

> the fear of formalisation and organisational change in congregations might be understood in the light of theories developed by Billis (1993) and Smith (1991) who argue that there are important organisational differences between membership associations and service-providing agencies.

> (Harris, 1995, p. 269)

ACCOUNTABILITY

The way in which organizational issues are handled will affect an organization's credibility. Because the Church is accountable through neither market forces nor the electoral process, it is the more desirable that it should consider the interactional nature of authority and the need to build in more specific means of accountability by those holding office.

The legitimacy of voluntary organizations has been identified with the notion of democratic accountability. However, it is important to distinguish between democracy and accountability. While there are limited empirical data examining accountability within the voluntary sector, it remains a useful means by which voluntary agencies can be made responsive to funders, beneficiaries and the public at large. The Church too may be seen to include funders, beneficiaries and the public at large, who may demand accountability as 'users', donors or volunteers. Unlike the Church, most voluntary organizations have clearly defined and publicized procedures for dealing with representations and complaints and they are regulated by the Charity Commission, who will respond to complaints from the public. The Church, which is also in receipt of large amounts of voluntary funding and is responsible in one way or another for large numbers of people, is not always clear about systems of accountability and would benefit from the establishment and development of standard procedures.

The effective voluntary agency is one in which aims and purposes are clearly defined, responsibilities appropriately designated and systems of accountability provided. Given our understanding of God and his mission of creation, how can structures of accountability be established within the Church which would enable clergy and laity to fulfil mutually appropriate roles? The existence of an independent voluntary governing body in the form of trustee or management committee is a distinct feature of the voluntary agency. Trustees are legally accountable for the organization and must attempt to balance competing and sometimes irreconcilable pressures.

A Church which preaches individual accountability at the last judgement needs to accept that its own actions as an organization should be open to scrutiny and challenge. Many New Testament passages attribute to Peter a particular responsibility for the mission, but it has been argued that while this function could be fulfilled by a single individual presiding over the whole Church it could also be carried out by a committee, board or synod.

However, the absence of a constitution for the Church enables 'a large measure of vagueness and flexibility' (Dulles, 1978, p. 55).

The starting point for accountability has been described as 'a construction of an agreed language or currency of discourse about conduct and performance and the criteria that should be used in assessing them'. In practice, the trustees of a voluntary organization can only govern with the consent of those governed. In much the same way as donors and users look to the governing body of a voluntary organization to answer for the agency's conduct, so the faithful have expectations of accountability in terms of the bishops. Voluntary organizations have developed appropriate organizational styles and structures to meet the requirements of organizational accountability (service delivery, campaigning, membership organizations, etc.). In the same way ecclesiastical structures need to be established in order to address the issue of accountability within the Church which transcends any moral duty of stewardship and becomes an essential prerequisite if the governing body is to continue to enjoy the authority which is afforded it.

Leat's description of the scope – fiscal, process, programme and priorities – of accountability provides a useful agenda for action. She distinguishes three different forms of accountability: the requirement to give an account; accountability with sanctions and responsive accountability. This third and weakest form of accountability pertains to the Church today and requires only that those who are accountable take into account or respond to the views or demands of those to whom they are accountable. However, although formal sanctions cannot be invoked, 'failure to be accountable in this sense, or to be responsive, may lead to loss of support from those who expect to have their views taken into account' (Leat, 1988, p. 20), and loss of financial support could be a major threat to the Vatican.

Given that the special service of the universal primate is 'to preside over the assembly of charity' and to foster collegial relationships among the regional bishops and particular churches, it has been argued that the concept of papal primacy should be interpreted to accord with a conciliar vision of the Church. The chair of trustees in a voluntary organization carries particular responsibilities but nevertheless remains a trustee among other trustees. The Pope, it is argued, also has special responsibilities but remains, with other bishops, a custodian of the organization.

GOVERNANCE AND AUTHORITY

'Order is heaven's first law.'

(Cited by Child, 1984)

To revert to the theories of Weber, it may be argued that the Church uses the two forms of authority:

1 *Traditional* and hierarchical, 'based on the belief in the sanctity of age-old rules and powers . . . the legitimating of present forms of domination achieved by reference to the past' (Lee and Newby, 1983, p. 181).
2 *Charismatic* authority, which is an original authority base and is currently seen at different levels within the Church. Such authority is entrepreneurial and arises from the 'particular qualities of an individual personality by virtue of which he is considered extraordinary and treated as endowed with supernatural, superhuman, or at least specifically exceptional powers or qualities' (Weber, 1968, p. 214).

The Church, however, operates in a world which has specific expectations of legitimate authority or rational legal authority and in which 'power' can be seen as a negative feature. Using organizational theory, power can be defined as the ability to exert influence in order to change attitudes and behaviour of individuals and groups. Authority, on the other hand, is a far more comfortable term and is seen as legitimate power, which contains the right to exert influence. In its turn, 'control' uses authority to ensure that actual activities conform to planned activities and helps to monitor progress and to evaluate and correct mistakes. Control within organizations is a process whereby management and other groups are able to initiate and regulate activities to meet the goals and expectations of the organization. Within the Church, control is highly centralized and formalized whereas many voluntary organizations are reviewing their way of operating in order to embody a more democratic notion of control which is based on delegation but uses an informal and self-regulatory system. However, inevitable tension lies in the fact that in many voluntary organizations control tends to be associated with resources.

Power in the Church tends to be a mixture of the traditional and the coercive or 'expert'. The former includes an appreciation of an 'external' source of power which is symbolic and far less tangible. Within the voluntary sector it is apparent that power, control and authority become issues when relationships are unclear, goals and authority are ill-defined, the structure is rigid and compromises unacceptable. They also become issues when lay people and clergy both want power and expect to exercise it. This can be a source of conflict; for example where the lay person has expert and referent power but the clergy possess authority.

In organizational terms, authority, power and control in a voluntary agency tend to lie ultimately with the board or management committee who are ultimately accountable for the agency. Voluntary sector theory identifies the board as a body of people carrying ultimate legal responsibility in relation to all aspects of the organization; members must be unpaid, without a statutory responsibility and must be the final point of accountability.

Most agencies within the Church will have a steering group or advisory committee. Diocesan and other church structures have a board of trustees in order to comply with Charity Commission registration criteria. Nevertheless, the relevance of such boards in terms of decision-making, policy-making or final accountability remains somewhat obscure. Within a voluntary agency, specific functions are undertaken by a board. Within the Church these are carried out indiscriminately by members of the hierarchy, e.g. policy-making and legal responsibility, the securing of resources, the selection and appointment of paid and voluntary staff, and representation of the agency to the local community and of the local community to the agency.

While this seems to conflict with voluntary sector practice, similar organization of governance and authority nevertheless exists within the voluntary sector and can be identified, explored and explained. Harris, for example, identifies the key players within an oganization as: the staff; clients/users; board/guardians/custodians; and the power relationship between them is the direct cause of particular benefits and difficulties in terms of authority and governance. The traditional model is one in which the custodians (G) form part of the board (B), which is where the authority lies. The board have power over the staff (S), who provide services for clients (C).

$$G \rightarrow B \rightarrow S \rightarrow C$$

Using this model, the governance relationship within the Church could be seen as 'the phantom board'. In this case the custodians or guardians govern the staff (clergy) who provide services for clients (the faithful). The 'board' has a tenuous link to the staff (clergy) and to the clients (faithful) but without clarification of responsibility or any indication of clear lines of communication.

G → S → C

B

In this context final accountability (power and authority) could be seen as 'external' and is inextricably linked to theological principles and a system of belief.

Conclusion

Such theories can begin to explain some of the unique and particular challenges facing both the Church and the voluntary sector. In his seminal report on the voluntary sector, more than twenty years ago, Wolfenden recommended that voluntary organizations should engage in active self-appraisal of their strategic activities and general effectiveness. A similar plea might be directed today towards the Church, whose internal workings and processes remain largely unexplored and unevaluated. The wider voluntary sector might indeed benefit from such research and thus the Church, as an organization, could be experienced and understood in a more liberating and fulfilling way and the proclamation of the gospel be better adapted to the world in which we live.

References

Bailey, D. (1992) 'The Strategic Restructuring of Non-profit Association', *Non-profit Management & Leadership* 3(1).

Billis, D. (1984) *Voluntary Sector Management*, Working Paper 1, CVO LSE.

Billis, D. (1993) *Organising Public and Voluntary Agencies*, Routledge.

Billis, D. and Glennerster, H. (1994) *Human Service Non Profits: Towards a Theory of Comparative Advantage*, LSE.

Billis, D. and Harris, M. (eds) (1996) *Voluntary Agencies: Challenges of Organisation and Management*, Macmillan.

Carr, W. (1985) *The Priestlike Task*, SPCK.

Child, J. (1985) *Organizations: A Guide to Problems and Practice*, Harper & Row.

Drucker, P. (1968) *The Practice of Management*, Pan.

Dulles, A., SJ (1978) 'Papal Authority in Roman Catholicism', in P. McCord (ed.), *A Pope for All Christians*, SPCK.

Handy, C. (1988) *Understanding Voluntary Organisations*, Penguin.

Harris, M. (1995) 'The Organisation of Religious Congregations: Tackling the Issues', *Non-profit Management & Leadership* 5(3).

Horton Smith, D. et al. (1980) 'The Non-profit Sector', in T. Connors (ed.), *The Non-profit Organisation Handbook*, McGraw Hill.

Kerkhofs, J. (ed.) (1995) *Europe Without Priests?* SCM.

Lash, N. (1977) *Voices of Authority*, Sheed & Ward.

Lauer, R. (1973) 'Organizational Punishment', *Human Relations* 26.

Leat, D. (1988) *Voluntary Organisations and Accountability*, NCVO.

Lee, D. and Newby, H. (1983) *The Problem Sociology*, Hutchinson.

Powell, W. and Friedkin, R. (1987) 'Organizing Change in Non-profit Organisations', in W. Powell (ed.), *The Non-profit Sector: A Research Handbook*, Yale University Press.

Weber, M. (1968) *Economy and Society*, Bedminster Press.

Wolfenden Report (1978) *The Future of Voluntary Organisations*, Croom Helm.

Young, D. (1989) 'Local Autonomy in a Franchise Age', *Non-profit & Voluntary Sector Quarterly* 18(2).

Zald, M. (1970) *Organizational Change*, Chicago University Press.

Chapter Five

THE EXPERIENCE OF WOMEN RELIGIOUS

Mary Linscott SND

Sister Mary Linscott, who belonged to the British Province of the Sisters of Notre Dame de Namur, died in 1999. She studied in Britain, France and the United States and had teaching and administrative experience at high school and college levels. From 1969 she served for nine years as Superior General, for eight of which she was President of the International Union of Superiors General, a capacity in which she attended three synods of bishops, was Consultor to the Council for the Laity, and was a member of the Commissions on the Holy Year of 1975 and on Women in the Church. Pope Paul VI appointed her to the Congregation for Religious and for Secular Institutes, where she was named head of office responsible for the approval of revised constitutions. In the course of this work, she had wide contacts with religious in different parts of the world and especially with English-speaking sisters. In November 1998, the French government made her a Chevalier de l'Ordre National du Mérite in recognition of her services to religious at the levels of both the local and the universal Church.

It is possible that the exercise of authority for governance in congregations of women religious of apostolic life may have something to offer to the faithful as a whole as one experience that touches the much wider question of authority in the Church. In this chapter I shall be dealing with five main areas:

1 The evolution of authority in religious life before the French Revolution.
2 Authority and governance in congregations of sisters prior to Vatican II.
3 Leadership and authority in renewal.
4 Authority for governance today.
5 The experience of sisters and the wider Church.

The Evolution of Authority in Religious Life Before the French Revolution

In the long history of religious life in the Latin Church, sisters are a recent development. There were anticipations at the time of the Counter-Reformation when pioneers such as St Angela Merici, St Alix le Clerq, St Jeanne de Lestonnac and Mary Ward envisaged a consecrated way of life for congregations of women who would be apostolically mobile. But these inspirations were ahead of their time, and the concept which they strove to express did not come into its own until the late eighteenth and early nineteenth centuries when the French Revolution and its aftermath swept away the kind of society which had to some extent shaped and supported previous forms of religious life and opened the way for new development. This period created at the same time a great range of new religious and social needs. The Holy Spirit responded by prompting a new form of consecrated life: women in a community living a vowed life in active service to the needy. During the industrial revolution and the successive waves of emigration in the nineteenth century the number of underprivileged people increased and the number of sisters increased alongside. There were, however, two persistent questions. The sisters were following Christ together and striving towards the fullness of his love by serving the needy: Were they truly religious, given that they had neither cloister nor solemn vows; and could they possess the necessary authority for governance for their scattered membership given that they were not exempt orders? The definitive answer came only in 1900, by which time practice was far ahead of legislation, as is often the case in the Church, and congregations of sisters had multiplied with unexpected rapidity. Prior to 1900 these earliest congregations found themselves outside church legislation, which had evolved over the centuries but had not envisaged their existence. As it stood, church legislation could not apply to them.

FORMS OF RELIGIOUS LIFE AND *CIRCA PASTORALIS*

Authority for governance developed with the different forms of religious life. The first of these was associated with the spontaneous movement of some Christians who, as the great Roman persecutions ended, gave one form of gospel witness by withdrawing to the desert as a substitute for martyrdom. Their call was often solitary: their life a combat with the forces of evil whose last stronghold was the wilderness. But among those who sought God in the desert were inevitably some who were experienced and others who were beginners. Without any structure and on an *ad hoc* basis, the learners seem to have turned to the wise for help on their personal journey to God. This suggests that, without organization, some of the desert fathers and mothers may have had a role of spiritual leadership, a kind of *de facto* authority based on competence and experience. The earliest elements of religious authority may, unconsciously, lie here – a mutual enablement in seeking God's will together in which the gifts of one are at the service of another in a way that helps both towards the fullness of vocation in Christ. This concept has remained a thread in the skein of religious authority down the centuries.

In a second phase, those wishing to live according to the ideals of the councils began to group together in monasteries – a development which not only required internal authority for the unity and organization necessary for the community, but also called for a formal recognition by the authority of the Church. By the fifth century the random multiplication of monks and monasteries presented such a problem that the Council of Chalcedon (451) acted on behalf of the Church universal – possibly the earliest instance of Church authority making an enactment with regard to religious life. The Council established the requirement of episcopal permission for the founding of a monastery and made monks subject to bishops. By the time that St Benedict (480–547), patriarch of western monasticism, was making his foundations, authority for religious governance had two aspects: the one internal to the monastery for its community affairs, and the other relating to the bishop and to the local and universal Church. Over a long period, the image of episcopal authority, which of its nature is hierarchical, came to affect the concept of the religious superior as father of his community. At times tension existed between the two aspects of authority. The balance between the authority necessary for internal governance and the authority of the bishop which was equally necessary for the good of the whole local Church became a constant topic of canonical legislation.

Then came the mendicants, who corresponded to the rise of mediaeval towns and universities and to the revival of commerce that followed the Crusades. Here the pattern of life was no longer the stability and close-knit unity of the monastery: the friar went about preaching the good news, begging his way, giving to the poor and belonging to a more flexible type of community. In order to function well, the mendicants needed structures of authority that gave a centralized kind of government. The need was handled not by adding appropriate legislation, but by extending a system of exemptions which already existed in the case of some large monasteries.

With the apostolic orders of the Counter-Reformation, the exempt religious became a form of religious life in themselves. The Jesuits are a good example of this development. Their basic need was not for stability but for apostolic mobility which would allow them to act in response to papal mandates, and they needed an authority and the structures of governance which would support far-flung commitments.

Ecumenical councils such as Constance (1414–18) and Lateran V (1512–17) tried to limit exemption and to iron-out conflicts of jurisdiction and authority that related to it. However, it was not until three years after the close of the Council of Trent that the decree *Circa Pastoralis* (1566) stated the basic law of the Church for religious, pulling together the canons of Lateran IV (1215), Lyons II (1274) and the 25th session of Trent itself. *Circa Pastoralis* tried to tidy up a complex and none-too-clear set of provisions and it did so in an honest if somewhat draconian manner. Religious were members of the Church living a common life with solemn vows and cloister. Historically exempt orders retained their exemptions. All but the exempt orders were under the jurisdiction of the local bishop. By implication, therefore, members of groups which were not cloistered, did not share a common life and did not take solemn vows were not religious. *Circa Pastoralis* is important because it virtually governed religious life until 1900. For historical reasons no ecumenical council took place between the end of the Council of Trent (1563) and Vatican I (1870), and in the years following the French Revolution – before the move to update and codify church law – the body of legislation and the jurisdiction of bishops no longer responded clearly to the actual developments in religious life. This period coincided with the foundation of many congregations of sisters.

ELEMENTS IN RELIGIOUS AUTHORITY

Three useful elements emerged from the long and chequered history of religious authority and governance prior to the nineteenth century. One was the ancient *de facto* authority of competence that went back to the desert fathers and mothers and found fresh expression in founders and foundresses down the years. Benedict, Francis, Ignatius, Angela and Mary Ward all possessed it in virtue of their vision and personal gifts and of their ability to attract others to their spirit and way of life. Such authority is personal and is not patient of legislation.

A second element is the authority which is necessary for unity, order and government and which, from approximately the fifth century, has been given by the Church in the form of approval of rules and constitutions and is increasingly in evidence when a religious group passes from the creative founding stage of light and fire to a consolidating stage that is more concerned with viability, development and maintenance. Always necessary for good functioning, this kind of authority derives from election or appointment to office. It is not personal in the sense of being an inalienable gift or charism though it is vested in persons. It can be legislated, it is limited in time and extent, and it is accountable. It is authority as of right – *ex officio* or *de jure*. Over the centuries, this form of authority came to loom much larger than the authority of competence and, on the eve of the French Revolution, its exercise was becoming increasingly confused with the power of office as the only models of ecclesial authority were bishops, many of whom were aristocrats working within an autocratic society.

The third element determining structures of authority for governance was perhaps the most significant from the point of view of sisters. This was the unique founding charism of each congregation. There was immense diversity ranging from the Benedictines at one end of an arc to the Jesuits at the other. The founding charism of St Benedict required an ordered life built around prayer and work and expressed in stability. Benedictines usually entered a particular monastery where they lived a stable, community life. They came to know their fellow religious, and had a pretty fair grasp of what was involved in governing the house; they could match persons to needs, and were rarely so numerous as to make community decisions difficult. This led to strong local government, and structures which provided for a high involvement of the members with a stress on elections and a steady use of community chapters.

The founding charism of Ignatius of Loyola was completely different. He certainly required an ordered life built around prayer and work, but he expressed it through a high degree of apostolic mobility. Jesuits did not enter a particular house or province, but the entire Society of Jesus. They had to be ready to move at short notice to wherever they were needed, and within the first fifty years this willingness led them to the countries of Europe, Africa, America and Asia. Jesuits needed to be able to take a great deal of personal initiative, always in the context of the discernment which was a hallmark of their spirituality. Apart from the first group who

were with Ignatius in Paris, there was no possibility of individual
Jesuits knowing in depth more than relatively few others. Nor
could they know of local conditions and needs in places as diverse
as Yamaguchi, Goa, Lisbon, London and the Great Lakes. In no
way could they match persons to jobs after the style of the Benedictines and they quickly became so numerous as to preclude decisions
taken by the whole body. Hence there developed a strong central
government balanced by structures within provinces and/or
regions, a clear chain of command and a great stress on communication. Response to the charism meant that each Jesuit had to be
known sufficiently well for him to be missioned responsibly to a
service for which he was equipped and in which he could grow.
This could not be done centrally, and different levels of authority
were set up: interrelated and complementary. Because of the priority of mobility, involvement of the individual in government was
largely by representation. Except in the election of the general, a
system of direct appointment rather than election was used to find
members to take responsibilities in government; councils rather
than chapters were the support groups for superiors at all levels.

Meanwhile the first congregations of sisters were still under *Circa
Pastoralis*, which allowed for two kinds of religious in the Church:
cloistered religious under the jurisdiction of the local bishop, and
the exempt orders such as the Jesuits, which were clerical. But the
sisters fell into neither category and set a high priority on apostolic
mobility. They had simple vows, their common life was not monastic, and they needed a kind of authority for government analogous
to that of the exempt orders. On the arc between Benedictine and
Jesuit patterns of government they would need to discover their
place in the light of their specific charism.

Authority and Governance in Congregations of Sisters prior to Vatican II

DEVELOPMENTS BEFORE 1900

The first wave of foundations of sisters was a phenomenon that the
corpus of church law could not have anticipated and for which
there was no provision. In the social upheaval of the French Revolution, interpretation of church law could vary widely. In the case of
my own congregation, founded in Amiens in 1804, the local bishop
took the view that, since church law said nothing about women religious of apostolic life, it was best to stick to *Circa Pastoralis*. Sisters
of Notre Dame should stay in the one diocese; there would be no

superior general; the bishop would have sole jurisdiction. But by 1808 the congregation was in four dioceses and had a superior general.

The bishops of Bordeaux, Ghent and Namur read the situation differently. For them the absence of canonical provision implied that there was nothing against the kind of life requested by the foundress, St Julie, and the first sisters. These bishops preferred to apply Gamaliel's principle and allow the life to prove itself. Meanwhile, they were prepared to support it. When the congregation was expelled from Amiens, it settled in Namur with a superior general and good relations with the local bishop.

This ambivalent situation under church law lasted throughout the nineteenth century. Church practice, however, was often ahead of legislation. In the case of my own congregation, Gregory XVI in 1844 had no hesitation 'with very great praise [in recommending] and by his apostolic authority [in approving] the said Institute as a Congregation of simple vows' despite the fact that it did not conform to *Circa Pastoralis* and that its constitutions (which he also approved) provided for government by a superior general. Thus the gap was steadily widening between church legislation and ordinary experience in religious life, and ecclesiastical authority, insofar as it understood what was going on, tried to bridge that gap by making individual exceptions. Because these were multiplying, some general legislation would probably have been on the agenda for Vatican I had the work of that council not been rudely interrupted by Garibaldi's march on Rome, and any clarification for sisters filed under 'unfinished business'. Congregations of women religious of apostolic life had to go on doing their best in a situation in which, technically, they were not religious and in which the approved model was mainly the cloistered one of *Circa Pastoralis*.

In these circumstances it was important that there should be an understanding of identity, charism and the living traditions in process of formation. In some congregations the traditions were strict, in others much more flexible. All carried the experience of the years before 1900 into the years of recognition and the Codes.

The majority of congregations of sisters were of European origin, coming into being as a response of the Spirit to the crying needs of nineteenth-century Europe. But it is characteristic of many that they quickly spread overseas. Sometimes in response to requests from missionary bishops in the Americas, Africa, Australia or the Far East, sometimes to accompany the waves of emigrants who left the European countries for America or the colonies. Sometimes it was to avoid persecution, as under the Kulturkampf in Germany or the Combes laws in France, and later in answer to a direct call from Rome when Pius XII appealed for foundations in Latin America. Some congregations spread widely. They took root in new cultures and tended to become international with the consequent need to keep a balance in government between the general and the local. They were established by the Apostolic See, were of pontifical right and were mainly accountable to the office of the Roman Curia whose most recent name is the Congregation for Institutes of Consecrated Life and Societies of Apostolic Life (CIVCSVA). Other religious congregations which grew up in particular countries were more local, and sometimes – but not always – smaller. They were established by the local bishop, were of diocesan right (canon 589) and were accountable to the local bishop. In either case 'a true autonomy of life, especially of governance [was] recognized for each institute'. As expressed much later in the Code of 1983 'this autonomy means that each institute has its own discipline in the Church and can preserve whole and entire its [unique, spiritual] patrimony' (canon 586, §1; cf. canon 578). The capacity for self-government in the religious sense is always a matter for attention in the giving of pontifical right to a petitioning congregation. Thus women religious of apostolic life, whether their congregation is of pontifical or of diocesan right, have authority given by the Church to govern themselves and they exercise it as lay religious.

CONDITAE A CHRISTO AND THE CODES OF CANON LAW 1917 AND 1983

The first notable step in the direction of recognition came in 1900 with Leo XIII's decree *Conditae a Christo* and the Norms which followed it in 1901. It made universal church law of what had been going on patchily for some time, by giving the right of self-government in accordance with approved constitutions to congregations who applied for it and who had already received a decree of praise.

Sisters were recognized as religious: a third form of religious life in the Church alongside those of *Circa Pastoralis* and the exempt orders. There was a great deal of unpacking still to be done, but the main idea was clear: authority was given so to govern as to attain the purpose for which the individual congregation was recognized by the Church. This meant that somehow authority was both ecclesial and congregational, structured in a form of government determined by the founding charism, accountable both to Church authority and to the congregation itself, and it was provided for in approved constitutions. This basic pattern has remained ever since.

This third form of religious life became canonical when the first Code of Canon Law was promulgated in 1917. This first Code still drew on the concept of the Church as a perfect society and perhaps reflected a certain ultramontane defensiveness in its legislation. It included the principles of *Conditae a Christo* but tended towards common concrete provisions and therefore to a certain uniformity. Many congregations revised their constitutions during the early 1920s as a result of the Code, and across these texts there is a high degree of similarity. The canons are extensively quoted with or without reference to source. There is a good deal of detail, much material reserved to ecclesiastical authorities, and the approach is not unlike that of Victorian elementary education: 'Do this as it is laid down and you will come to the values and principles later.' The model for religious was basically – but perhaps unconsciously – monastic, and this later gave rise to tension within congregations of apostolic life because the provisions of the Code were stable, particularly those dealing with community life, while the mission itself was mobile and developing and sisters presenting themselves as candidates had had the benefit of an education and experience hardly thought of in 1917. Models for the exercise of authority still reflected the idea of power with which church authority had come to be associated over several centuries, and the interpretation of the role of canonical superior could sometimes result in an authoritarian style of operation.

To move ahead for a moment, it should be stated that many of the weaknesses of the Code of 1917 were redressed by the revised version of 1983. Between the two stood the whole experience of the Second Vatican Council with its different idea of Church, its recognition and stress on the diversity of founding gifts and its strong concept of authority as service. For John Paul II, the revised Code was, so to speak, the final document of the Council. Its recognition that religious were in an age of evolution rather than in a fixed state was important for sisters. Although some matters were still reserved to church authorities a great many were now referred to the congregations themselves, by comparison with 1917. The pedagogic principle of 1917 was also reversed. The Code of 1983 preferred broad values: 'Here are broad values and principles; you discover how to live them.'

On one point, however, the Codes caused confusion. Whether it meant to do so or not, the Code of 1917 seemed to imply three states in the Church: clerical, religious and lay. According to canon 491 of that document, religious took precedence over the laity though they themselves were not clerics. Given the high visibility of sisters at the time, and of congregations of brothers who were in a similar situation, the general perception was of three states, and sixty years later the distinctions were firmly established. The revised Code of 1983, however, clearly envisages only two states and defines religious negatively:

> In itself the state of consecrated life is neither clerical nor lay. A clerical institute is one which ... is under the governance of clerics, presupposes the exercise of sacred orders and is recognized as such by ecclesiastical authority. A lay institute is one which is recognized as such by ecclesiastical authority because ... its proper role ... does not include the exercise of sacred orders.
>
> (canon 588 §§1–3)

All women religious of apostolic life, like their cloistered sisters and congregations of brothers, are therefore members of lay institutes, a fact which since *Christifideles Laici* has led in some cases to confusion of identity as the idea of a lay religious did not sit easily with the categories of thought of the previous half-century. Nevertheless, sisters are canonically recognized as members of lay institutes and it is as lay religious that they are expected to govern themselves.

AUTHORITY FOR GOVERNANCE ON THE EVE OF THE SECOND VATICAN COUNCIL

In the early 1960s, authority for government was not a major issue in congregations of sisters. The nature and source of such authority was not examined and authority itself was assumed rather than defined. There were few questions about it. The issue of authority for governance did not loom large in proposals made for special general chapters (1966–70), and the existing situation seemed adequate for a way of life which had not been under close scrutiny for generations.

Leadership and Authority in Renewal

THE MANDATE

The mandate of Vatican II to religious was deceptively mild: an up-to-date renewal of the life and discipline of each congregation in accordance with the gospel, the supreme rule, the spirit and aims of the founder, the initiatives of the Church, contemporary conditions and genuine spiritual renewal. Telescoped into the slogan 'the gospel, the charism and the signs of the times' was a programme which the council fathers probably anticipated in terms of a review of life followed by appropriate adjustments. The effect was more like touching off a fuse. In terms of authority and government, the Council called for anything obsolete to be dropped, and the introduction of necessary changes, and encouraged the conciliar principles of subsidiarity, participation and co-responsibility. There was an emphasis on the involvement of members, and the tone was given in n. 18 of *Ecclesiae Sanctae*:

> The mode of government should be such that 'chapters and councils should express, each one at its own level, the involvement and the concern of all the members of the community for the good of the whole' (*Perfectae Caritatis*, n. 14). This will be the case, especially, if the members have a real and effective part in the choice of chapter and council officials. Again, the mode of government should be such that the exercise of authority is rendered more effective and expeditious, as our times demand. Superiors, therefore, at every level should be given appropriate powers, so as to minimize unnecessary or too frequent recourse to higher authority.

Such a mandate would have had an impact on sisters anyway. They were in the habit of taking up ecclesial initiatives and many of them plunged into renewal as an act of faith. But in their case the conciliar directives were programmed with an unusual concreteness as regards procedure. Like all religious, sisters were not only encouraged to renew themselves, but were mandated to do so by means of specific procedures and to deadlines. The Council clearly meant something to happen! The decree enjoining renewal, *Perfectae Caritatis* (28 October 1965), was followed on 6 August 1966 by norms for its implementation, *Ecclesiae Sanctae*. The norms prescribed that in order 'to put renewal and adaptation into effect, a special general chapter is to be summoned within two or at the most three years'. This chapter was special in that it could be divided into two sessions provided that not more than a year elapsed between one session and the next and provided also that the chapter itself decided in favour of this by secret ballot. More importantly it had the special faculty of being able to sanction experiments that did not harmonize with existing constitutions without having recourse to ecclesiastical authorities, though it could not contravene canon law. Such a chapter was to be prepared by an unprecedented involvement of the sisters: as the norms state, 'the general council must arrange for an ample and free consultation of all the members with results available in good time to guide and assist the work of the chapter'.

A period of experimentation was foreseen which was to last from the end of the special general chapter to the next ordinary chapter following it and, where necessary, to the chapter following that one. This meant that the time of experimentation would vary according to the frequency of general chapters in a given congregation. For most sisters, the period of experimentation would cover about twelve years. At the end of that time, each congregation was to re-present its constitutions revised in the light of the experience of renewal to the appropriate ecclesiastical authority. All very tidy; but it turned out to be anything but the peaceful revision anticipated.

THE TIMING

Ecclesiae Sanctae was nearer the truth than it knew when it pronounced that: 'Suitable renewal cannot be achieved once and for all: it needs to be fostered continually.' Sisters passed from a static understanding of authority to a much more dynamic one and to an ongoing rethinking of government largely because the lapidary conciliar mandate coincided with other forces moving them towards organic change. For sisters, the Council's directive came at an historically ripe moment. Not only were they becoming increasingly aware of the internal tension between the original vision of their congregations and current assumptions regarding their legislation, but the educational movement of the 1950s had prepared a higher proportion of them to reflect on the issues and to articulate them. The Council required that these issues be addressed, and promptly. The result was a total re-examination of life. It coincided with the communications and technological explosion of the 1960s, with the authority crisis in society and in the Church, with the increasing influence of the human sciences, with the accelerated emergence of the feminist movement and with conscientization in areas such as justice and peace, human dignity, global awareness and their opposites: social oppression, discrimination, violence, racism, hunger. Because of their involvement with society, sisters found that many of these elements affected the way that they went about renewal. Certainly they affected the sisters' eventual rethinking of authority and governance which emerged as a critical area once the congregations arrived at the stage of revising their constitutions.

THE EXPERIENCE

Inevitably sisters went first for adaptation rather than renewal. Adaptation meant concrete changes that could be made and seen: structures, processes, dress, lifestyle, distribution of resources. In the course of coming to grips with these, new leaders began to emerge who we could call natural, charismatic or 'born' leaders – not unlike the very early authorities of competence among the desert religious. But now the competence tended to be in a particular professional field, in an ability to communicate or in a good grasp of dynamics. Whatever the gift, this kind of leader tended to come to the fore at the expense of leadership based on *ex officio* authority and experience of government. Moreover, as a result of the conciliar requirement of a wide involvement of the membership, general chapters from 1967 onwards were of a different composition from those which went before. There was less experience of the exercise of government and more creativity; less hard information and more 'dreaming' in the positive sense; less history and more social analysis; less theology and more impact from the human sciences. All these elements were potentially good but needed to be balanced if they were to lead to good religious government. A time of struggle, confusion and emotion is not the best moment for balancing, and the difficult years of the 1970s and early 1980s did not allow time for evaluation. There was a lack of the necessary distance for objectivity. The individualism of the time produced leaders in plenty without a corresponding number of sisters willing to accept responsibility. Expectations were not clear. Both constitutions and the Code of Canon Law were under revision and it was far easier to raise questions than to find constructive responses. At the same time, there was the very strong backlash from what was perceived as pre-Vatican authoritarianism which made the very word authority politically incorrect, and greatly increased the difficulties of government. There was an awareness of the fall in overall numbers of vocations, of the increased number of departures, of the new needs that were multiplying and could not be met. And of the fact that in several countries the state was taking over the long-standing institutionalized works formerly done by religious. There was, too, the sense of being a microcosm of a Church and world which were also in flux and seeking their way.

The need to blend the enabling leadership of competence with the right exercise of legitimate authority began to emerge as adaptation slowly gave way to the deeper matter of renewal – an ongoing permanent inner conversion affecting beliefs, values, attitudes, commitment and relationships. The very fact that leadership as such is a gift which is neither predictable nor controllable from the point of view of legislation means that, in government, it needs a balance which can be predicted and legislated. That balance was seen in terms of authority. In the years following the Second Vatican

Council, the balance afforded by *ex officio* authority was significantly down-played, mainly as a reaction to authoritarianism, and also because of the trend towards greater participation. By the late 1980s the bulk of the revised constitutions had been presented, and it was evident that greater participation does not remove the need for authority; that authoritarianism is an abuse which can be handled without touching the principle of authority itself; and that in the case of religious both participation and authority relate closely to the vow of obedience which has itself been under review since the Council.

Authority for Governance Today

The internal exercise of authority for governance in congregations of women religious of apostolic life is different today. Prior to the Vatican Council and *Perfectae Caritatis*, such exercise had to some extent reflected the patterns of authority in the hierarchical Church. Offices could be for life. There were various levels in practice. Authority could count on obedience for acceptance. It was assumed but not evaluated. There was little critique or updating of structures. Although sisters had not only the right but the duty to represent whatever might be to the good of the congregation, authority moved from the top down.

During the past thirty years, much of this has been modified. In a broad sense, terms of office are limited by the Code and, specifically, by the provisions of constitutions. The various levels of government remain but always with an accountable subsidiarity and with many more decisions referred to intermediate units. The membership is widely involved and, while obedience is still there, great attention is given to the sisters' 'owning' decisions. Critique and evaluation are constant. After a short period in which the theory of 'authority being in the membership' seemed to overlook the ecclesial dimension completely, the right blend is still being sought between authority coming from the top down and authority coming from the grassroots up. Part of the difficulty today is that sisters' experience of authority and governance bears less resemblance to the previously perceived values, processes and structures of hierarchical authority. Religious are not part of the Church's hierarchical structure. They have had to find their own models and, in fact, were mandated to do so. It is not surprising that sisters come up with something which is a distinct development from their past history and more in accordance with the signs of the times, and it is important that this should not be seen as some form of disloyalty to the Church, but the very opposite. Whether aware of it or not, sisters have moved along the Church's own line of growing self-understanding since the great Latin-American conferences at Medellín (1967), Puebla (1979), and Santo Domingo (1983): mystery, communion and mission, the people of God in all its dimensions building what Paul VI described as the civilization of love.

This has not happened without mistakes along the way. An outstanding one was a failure to make the necessary link between authority, government structures and the founding charism. What had been lucidly clear to founders and foundresses was much less so to chapter members in 1966, and they did not yet have Cardinal Hume's admirable presentation on charisms in his opening discourse to the synod of 1994. The result was a tendency for ideas about government to cross uncritically from one congregation to another, especially via the various national conferences of religious, and for sisters to confuse values and structures necessary for stability with those required for their own apostolic mobility. The mistake did not lie in whether or not there should be participation and coresponsibility but in how these should be worked out in practice. The 'how' should not, for example, exclude some members from exercising their right to vote by requiring their physical presence at assemblies, nor should it fail to get the right sisters into the right jobs by relying too much on volunteering. Meetings should not be multiplied unnecessarily by requiring them for trivial agenda, and decisions for the wider mission need not be handicapped by internal differences of opinion that are thought to need consensus. All these areas had to improve with experience.

Another difficult area lay in over-dependence on models which did not involve faith, vows or Church and whose goals differed from those of religious congregations. Organization, management and administration all come into the exercise of authority for religious governance, but they fall short of that which is essential to it. It was not wise, therefore, to stress in an absolute way ideas coming from the world of commerce or politics, however interesting and illuminating these might be in themselves.

There may also have been a too-slow appreciation of the connection between authority for governance and changes taking place in life and in works. Pre-Vatican II governmental structures corresponded on the whole to rather large centralized communities and to well-established, viable, institutionalized, corporate works. All this was changed by the dramatic fall in numbers of sisters, the weighting of the age-graph towards the upper decades, and the taking over by the state of responsibilities in education, health and social work which in earlier years had fallen to sisters. Communities became small and scattered, with the exception of a few much larger ones for the sick and the aged. Works were more individualized. In many cases authority at local level was no longer effective. All this affected structures for government and such structures were slow in adaptation.

After several generations of viability in which relevance was never under discussion because the needs of society were so evident, there was a period in which some congregations experienced a lack of confidence in the validity of their own founding gifts. This was a circumstance rather than a mistake. Following the appearance of *Christifideles Laici* in 1988, 23 years after the launching of renewal, some sisters went through a kind of crisis of identity. They either perceived themselves in a negative light or saw no difference between their post-conciliar life and the lives of the laity. The concept and experience of authority had little to do with the minor wave of departures at this time.

On the positive side of the scale, a 1992 study of a cross-section of 60 sets of revised constitutions presented in English brought out the elements that marked the current phase of authority for governance:

- A clear sense that religious authority has its source in Christ himself and is to be exercised as he exercised it: as service, and for his purposes. Authority is both of the Church and of the congregation though its nature and source are not worked out.
- A sharp awareness of rediscovered founding charisms as determining structures of authority.
- The concept of complementary necessary gifts between the sister exercising authority and the members of her council or team.
- The concept that the fostering of the diversity of gifts in the membership is a key responsibility of authority for governance.
- Openness to a wide involvement of the sisters in government according to their roles and experience, continuing the conciliar thrust concerning the dignity of each person and expressing the belief that the Holy Spirit can work through each for the good of the whole.
- The adoption of shared responsibility, subsidiarity and accountability as basic principles;
- The avoidance of any idea of we/they in speaking of authority and membership.
- The recognition by many of the link between authority for government and the vow of obedience: a link which draws on faith

and on relationship to the Church and which ultimately distinguishes religious authority from administration, organization,
management, or indeed any other form of governance.
- The wide adoption of processes of consensus and discernment,
  variously understood.

The present situation is not the last word. With the rest of the
Church, sisters are involved in ongoing renewal as a way of life and
ongoing conversion. They are not moving from one pre-Vatican
fixed point to another somewhere after the millennium. They do
not know what their future will be. There are areas which need
very much more attention, such as the nature and source of their
authority for governance, the question of authority coming from
the top down and/or from the grassroots up (why and why not),
the structures required to meet radical changes in lifestyles and
works. Yet, despite the suffering and effort of the past thirty years –
perhaps even because of them – there is a learning process under
way in faith: learning amid a fair amount of trial and error, and
with varying mixes of tension, resistance, courage and joy, but with
a seemingly inexhaustible fund of good will.

Sisters' Experience and the Wider Church

It remains to be seen whether or not and to what extent the sisters' experience of authority for governance may be of help to the wider
Church at a time which is characterized by the emergence of the
laity. Granted that charisms, including the founding gifts of religious
congregations, are given not only for the immediate recipients but in
view of the upbuilding of the Church as a whole, and that religious
congregations are to some extent a microcosm of the whole Church,
there may well be some relationship between the experience of
sisters and that of the faithful at large. There are issues and questions
which may have common elements for sisters and for the laity as
members of the one Church. The approach is not a stratification of
levels but the interrelation of different parts of the one body of Christ.

A clarification of authority had to take place before constitutions
were re-presented for approval in the 1980s. The terms 'leadership'
and 'authority' had been used interchangeably with confusing
results, until it emerged that authority for governance is largely
understood by sisters in terms of the authority which is given by the
Church in the recognition of the congregation and the approval of
the constitutions. It is an authority closely linked with the vow
of obedience and is proper to those living a consecrated life: it is

internal to each congregation and it is *ex officio*. In the course of renewal, however, two further concepts emerged: leadership (akin to the old authority of competence), which in some areas was put forward as a substitute for *ex officio* authority; and the 'authority of membership' which expressed the desire to balance any hierarchical structure with total involvement of all the members irrespective of roles. The last two could relate to authority and governance and the laity, as leadership is a human gift present in the laity as in the rest of the Church: a charism that can be given to anyone. The question of authority of membership goes deeper. It raises the question of the royal people of God. Is there an authority that attaches to baptism because it admits a person to the holy, priestly and royal people of God, sharing the role of Christ who is king as well as priest and prophet? Does such authority exist and if so in what form? How does it relate to the *ex officio* or *de jure* authority for government which is vested in the Church's hierarchy and in lawfully elected or appointed superiors in religious congregations?

A second issue concerned the question of whether authority came only from the top down or whether it could also come from the grass-roots up. This issue was exacerbated by the fact that the period of post-Vatican renewal coincided with the years when democracy was being hailed as the one acceptable and desirable form of government for everyone. Political and cultural influences were strong. When the Council opened up the concept of the Church as the whole people of God there was a move towards the kind of involvement of the whole which would have made the Church a kind of democracy. Which it is not. One very real question for the Church was that of how to involve all the members in ways that respect human dignity and the presence of the Spirit in all the baptized without infringing the authority that Christ thought necessary for the unity and mission of the whole. And that question was present in microcosm in religious congregations alongside two related questions: that of the right to dissent – an insistent issue in the 1980s; and the question of the extent to which authority is becoming increasingly dependent for effectiveness on the ownership of decisions by members. Both are live issues whether they concern a congregation of sisters or members of the laity. In some way two extremes have to be avoided: on the one side processes and structures must not atrophy, on the other a new understanding must not destroy the nature of religious authority itself or create a situation in which it is no longer possible to exercise it. Perhaps we might move the question from the context of political democracy, where it is often found, to that of faith, where it truly belongs. It then becomes not an either/or but a matter of the pooling and exchange of gifts which respects hierarchical authority while fully recognizing and fostering the input and experience of religious and laity that are necessary in order to exercise authority with a good grasp of current reality.

Sisters, especially those belonging to international congregations, reflect a broader situation regarding authority in the Church in terms of the relationship between centralization and diaspora. Early missions overseas were founded with great generosity and good will but with a practical mentality which was sometimes colonial. With Vatican II and the much greater insertion of sisters into society, there came inculturation and the so-called cycle of mission: missionaries sent to an unevangelized area first took the lead but then worked in tandem with the new local church and, in a third stage, handed over responsibility for it to the members of the new church. In the case of sisters founding new provinces, this led relatively quickly to the need to distinguish between unity and uniformity. Styles of exercising authority had to become more flexible and the relationship between the generalate and the provinces had to be rethought. In the name of subsidiarity much was delegated to provinces in the immediate aftermath of the Council since, without a revision of over-centralized structures, the congregations would not have been able to operate. But by 1990 there had to be a second look at the role of the generalate in the interests of unity. This is a far more complex and important area today than was previously the case. It is a prime field for ongoing discernment since it involves the full appreciation of the work of the Spirit in the richness of outlying diversity as well as the unifying work of that same Spirit at the centre. The interaction between centre and diaspora is vital, whether between a sisters' generalate and its provinces or between Rome and the local churches.

In the experience of post-conciliar authority for governance, sisters have had to deal with phenomena that are by no means peculiar to themselves. Three such phenomena are worth noting:

1 Progress in adapting authority structures to the Council's requirements of subsidiarity, co-responsibility and participation. All members had to be involved if such progress was to be successful, but such involvement was rarely uniform or smooth. Positions were taken on the extreme right or the extreme left, both in the name of the same founding charism, and in ways which would damage the charity of a congregation: each extreme digging in its heels. Between the two extremes there was often a large group of moderate sisters whose voices were insufficiently heard. This

kind of thing happened with a remarkable frequency across many congregations. The voiceless moderates were important, but not easy to reach.

2 The speed of change between 1965 and 1997 has been unprecedented. Any five-year period demonstrated greater differences than had been previously experienced within a generation or more. It was not possible to count for long on the capital of a stable tradition as sisters who had experienced such stability were steadily being replaced by those who knew only flux and change.

3 The search for new forms of consecrated life, sparked by the careful reference to their possibility in canon 605. This led to new initiatives regarding associates and co-workers, volunteers and part-time collaborators and could range from a revival of the mediaeval third orders expressed in apostolic terms, to the establishment of groups that were more like the lay movements such as the Focolarini, the neo-catechumenal way, Communion and Liberation, St Egidio. The new initiatives usually addressed works as well as spirituality. They were a fresh expression of the original charism of the congregation. They did not involve authority to the same extent as government of vowed religious, but often helped the congregation with which they were associated to think through its own identity more clearly.

The Second Vatican Council was a watershed for sisters in terms of the exercise of authority. The stress on diversity of gifts, on authority as service, and on the involvement and co-responsibility of the members of each congregation in government according to their various roles, led to changes that are still being worked through and required evaluation. Those changes lie to a great extent in the areas of processes, communication, structures and style. Necessary to a right evaluation is a clearer grasp of some deeper aspects of the authority necessary for religious governance: research which has still to be undertaken. Such aspects include:

1 The nature of religious authority in the congregation and in the Church.

2 The source or sources of such authority.

3 The connection between religious authority and the vow of obedience.

4 The relationship between religious authority and the royal character of all the baptized and the relationship between religious authority and the jurisdiction of the hierarchy.

Sisters have particular experience to bring to the area of governance and this could well be enlarged upon in consultation with other traditions: monastic observance, clerical institutes, congregation of brothers, secular institutes and societies of apostolic life.

Why did the question of authority for governance catch fire so quickly among sisters after 1966? Leaving aside for the moment the convergence of circumstances which made the conciliar programme of renewal so timely, a determining factor lay in the strength and practicality of the Council's mandate to religious. I wonder whether the renewal of religious life would have proceeded so vigorously if the council fathers had been content with exhortations. As it was, the mandate spelled out specifically what had to be done, by what means, within what timescale and the question of accountability. It gave a very tight deadline. Given the attitude of religious to the ecclesiastical authorities of the time, that was more than enough to produce action: unexpected and largely unprepared but nevertheless universal and effective. By and large action was taken in line with the Council's recommendations and was somehow for the good of the whole Church as well as for the sisters themselves. As far as I am aware there was nothing to parallel this concrete mandate in the provisions made for the hierarchy or for the laity. In the context of the Church as the whole people of God, it remains to be seen whether or not the experience of sisters can be of use in updating the exercise of authority for governance in the Church of our changing times.

Chapter Six

WHAT FUTURE FOR THE LAITY? LAW AND HISTORY

Robert Ombres OP

Fr Robert Ombres OP was born in Naples in 1948, and came to England as a child. He studied law at the universities of Bristol and London, and became a barrister. Having become a friar in the Dominican Order, he was ordained priest in 1976. He studied theology at Blackfriars, Oxford, and canon law in Rome. After spells as Prior in Cambridge and Oxford, he is now a member of Oxford University's theology faculty. He has written on and teaches canon law and moral theology. He has just coedited the volume *English Canon Law* (Cardiff, 1998).

> If the Church, secure on her foundations, boldly throws herself open to lay activity, she will experience such a springtime as we cannot imagine.
> Cardinal Yves Congar

Introduction

'Authority', especially in a Christian context, is a far wider term than 'governance'. I have concentrated on authority in the sense of governance because the power of governance has daily repercussions at all levels of the Church, from what the Pope does through the Roman Curia to what the parish priest decides.

The focus will be on the power to govern, part of the 'royal' dimension of the triple office of Christ as priest, prophet and king. The task is to see how this dimension is shared and distributed within the Church. By baptism, each believer has some share in all three dimensions. My aim is to isolate the one sphere, that of 'kingship', and to explore historically how it is shared between clerics and lay people. Authority in the Church has been, and must be, approached from multiple points of view, each enriching the others. One of these points of view needs to be that of law, as authority in the Church is both understood and carried out in juridical ways. Also, as will emerge, today's canon law was intended to be the juridical expression of Vatican II's ecclesiology.

91

Canon law itself has not been understood in the same fashion at all times, and moreover the relationship of canon law to other dimensions of Christianity has not been the same. This is vital to the topic of authority. A glance at the New Testament, at the early collections of laws, at Gratian, at the Decretals and other medieval papal documents, and at the varying styles of conciliar decrees and texts, will bear out this diversity. Above all, history throws into sharp relief how significant the twentieth century has been in terms of the Church's canonical self-understanding. This has been the century of codifications and it has been a revolution.

Popes, as supreme legislators, promulgated *codes* of canon law in 1917 and in 1983 for the Latin Church and in 1990 for the Eastern Catholic Churches. This had never been done before, and the repercussions are great. Marking a break with tradition, which consisted in the accumulation over centuries of a body of canon law (*Corpus Iuris Canonici*), the era of codification (*Codices Iuris Canonici*) begun in 1917 centralized authority greatly, reduced the influence of law-creating agencies other than the papacy, favoured highly abstract conceptual statements, placed interpretation and development firmly with the Roman authorities, and inevitably reduced the influence of custom as expressed by Christian communities and by local ecclesiastical judges.

Canon law is an important expression of authority in the Church, but the revolution of codifying this law has affected how authority is understood and exercised. It inevitably centralized authority and made it more firm, more enforceable universally, more standardized. A varied, piecemeal *body* of canonical documents is more diffuse, less open to central control, more responsive to differences in time and place. Codification tends to favour the statement of what look like absolute and clear norms. Yet because canon law is not isolated in the life and theology of the Church, a mystery only open to partial understanding, it should be more responsive to other dimensions. Codified canon law favours certainty, while in important respects a full theological understanding may not be available.

Codification tends to ignore history, with its complications and diversities. Thus since 1917 canon law studies have been dominated by the exegesis of the text of the Codes with the consequence that the main sources of canon law (the scriptures and tradition in a wide sense) had been put at a fair remove from statements of the law as it is at any given time.

As canon law is basically applied ecclesiology, law in general – and codified canon law in particular – expresses and reinforces a particular model of the Church. In a Church such as the Latin Church, whose heritage and self-understanding has acquired over the centuries a markedly legal flavour, authority will inevitably have strong juridical connotations. The history of the Church and its theologies (note the plural) do not however show that authority needs inevitably to be understood in a way encouraged by twentieth-century codification.

Canon Law

In the Church, especially in the Latin Church, authority is in important respects worked out and understood juridically.

What is the present canonical understanding of authority and governance in the Church as it affects the laity?

Book II of the 1983 Code, which attempts to express canonically the ecclesiology of Vatican II, is headed 'The People of God'. There it is made clear (canon 204) that the people of God is made up of the baptized faithful. Each and every one of the faithful participate in their own way in the priestly, prophetic and kingly office of Christ. Being Church is not, therefore, simply a sociological grouping, neither can office be understood simply in terms of organizational models, power politics, or secular analogues. Office in the Church, whoever has it, is a participation in *Christ's* office. Authority in the Church must therefore be discussed theologically, within which global understanding other levels can take their place.

By 'the faithful' the Code does not mean the laity. It means *all* baptized. There is a genuine equality of dignity and action among all of Christ's faithful. Because of this equality (canon 208), all the faithful contribute, each according to his or her own condition and office, to the building up of the body of Christ. An important, divinely willed distinction among Christ's faithful is, however, that between clerics and laity (canon 207). To put it graphically, almost as a mathematical formula:

$$CHURCH = FAITHFUL \ (CLERICS + LAITY)$$

and not

$$CHURCH = CLERICS + LAITY$$

The consequences of this are far-reaching. The Code gives a list of the duties and rights which belong to all the faithful, and then continues in separate sections to specify duties and rights according to whether they belong to clerics or to lay people. There are three terms, then, not two. The broad category is that of the faithful, who are specified as either clergy or laity. But both clerics and lay people never cease to belong to the faithful. We can now avoid the clerical/lay polarization by seeing the underlying category of 'the faithful' as fundamental.

The power of governance, also called jurisdiction, is said (para. 1 of canon 129) to belong to the Church by divine institution, and that it is clerics who are capable of it. The second paragraph adds that lay members of Christ's faithful can cooperate in the exercise of the same power in accordance with the law. Theologically, therefore, the power of governance which lies with the faithful is fulfilled by those in sacred orders, who have the capacity to do it. The power of governance is divided into legislative, executive and judicial power (canon 135).

History

If this is an accurate sketch of how authority and governance are understood canonically in the Latin Church, how does this current understanding fit into the Church's history of almost two millennia?

As we have seen, canon law has not had the same function in the Church over the centuries, and different understandings of law in the Church affect how authority is understood and exercised. It seems accurate to say also that the legal dimension of authority (in an increasing positivist sense) has not always been present in the Church in the same fashion. Above all, and this affects the primacy of Peter and his successors, the juridical and sacramental elements were dissociated from an earlier closer relationship. The office-holder grew more isolated from dependence on a whole ecclesial context of believers, including obviously the laity.

What then of the pivotal canon 129? It is categorical that clerics are capable of the power of governance or jurisdiction (*potestas regiminis* or *jurisdictionis*) whilst lay people can cooperate in its exercise.

In the earlier parts of the Middle Ages, various terms were used to designate the power of church leaders: *potestas, auctoritas, cura animarum, ius, regimen* and *iurisdictio* among them. As canonists grew more independent of their secular colleagues, we can perhaps identify the emerging importance of *iurisdictio*, a term which does not seem to figure centrally before the thirteenth century. It was used increasingly to mean public power. It could be argued that a term with more religious connotations was better suited to the renewed vision of the Church after Vatican II. No doubt as yet another compromise, the term *iurisdictio* is in canon 129, but it comes after the term *regimen*, which is a more neutral-sounding term and one close to

Vatican II's *munus regendi*. The current canon 129§1 is based on canon 196 of the 1917 Code, which also had the two terms but placed *iurisdictio* before *regimen*.

It could well be a sign of unease in all this, made sharper by greater historical awareness, that while the 1983 Code has a separate Book on the teaching office of the Church (Book III on the *munus docendi*) and a separate Book on the sanctifying office of the Church (Book IV on the *munus sanctificandi*) it does not have a separate Book on the governing office of the Church (the *munus regendi*).

In the long and varied history of the Church, the Reformation and its aftermath had consequences on how the Church viewed its authority and power. Given the nature of the Reformation, the clerical element and above all the papacy were given polemical emphasis. The story did not end there. When canon 129 says that the power of governance in the Church is instituted by God (*'quae quidem ex divina institutione est in Ecclesia'*) we cannot help recalling sharp conflicts from the past.

The present canon more or less repeats canon 196 of the 1917 Code, behind which there stands a 1794 constitution of Pius VI, a document from the Roman Curia of 1797 and an encyclical letter by Pius X from 1907. To see their relevance we need to reconstruct the effect on the Church's understanding of power, and clerical power at that, produced by reaction to the Council of Pistoia (1786), the crisis over Modernism early in the twentieth century, together with the French Revolution and its anti-clerical aftermath. Pius VI condemned as heresy (1794) any notion of the power of governance coming 'from below', from the community of the faithful.

Soon after this condemnation, Rome was declared a republic and Pius VI taken abroad as a captive, so that the notion of 'liberty, equality and fraternity', the new ideas of constitutional rule and popular sovereignty, associated with the French Revolution, could hardly find a ready welcome in the Church.

This tension between the Church and the various important strands of post-revolutionary thought in Europe is involved in any discussion of the laity's authority in the Church. Thus, for example, supporters of the nineteenth-century 'trustees system' in the USA thought of the extension of lay control over church matters as a working out of the principles of 'liberty and equality'. It is significant that the most pivotal canon we have, canon 129§1, has no source assigned to it except canon 196 of the 1917 Code; nothing at all from Vatican II. In turn, the 1917 canon had as its two main sources a 1794 condemnation of one proposition attributed to the council of Pistoia (1786) and a general reference to the entire encyclical *Pascendi* (1907), part of the anti-Modernist campaign. The years 1794 and 1907 were not ideal for balanced theological reflection in Rome on the authority of the laity!

Returning to canon 129, it states boldly that it is clerics who are capable of being given the power of governance, of jurisdiction. This link between the sacrament of order and the power of governance is an ancient one in the Church but also complex and controversial. Cardinal Ratzinger, commenting on the *Nota praevia* of Vatican II, reflected that the question concerning the powers of order and jurisdiction was one of the thorniest legal and constitutional problems in all the history of the Church. It raises the delicate matter of 'absolute' ordinations, that is ordinations without specific authority over something or someone.

Lumen Gentium nn. 8 and 21 have not solved everything, and the latter deals only with episcopal ordination in any case. But our focus is on the laity, although their position will only make complete sense in a context that includes clerics and indeed the Church as a whole. A further complication arises when we recall that while today the 'cleric' is someone who has been ordained deacon, presbyter or bishop, historically the term has been much wider and has included all kinds of 'minor orders'. Now, all clerics are ordained in the fullest sense, i.e. as deacon, presbyter or bishop. But in the past what was the nature of clerical authority? Furthermore, the position of the deacon is a complication as he is ordained a cleric but not sacerdotally. Also involved is the relationship of the priesthood shared by everyone through baptism to the ministerial priesthood given at ordination. *Lumen Gentium* n. 10 is firm on this, and adds that the ministerial priesthood, through the sacred power (*sacra potestas*) it has, forms and governs (*'regit'*) the priestly people.

Canon 129§2 does, then, go on to say that lay people can cooperate in the exercise of the power of governance, of jurisdiction, held by clerics. What of this? It is a long and unfinished story which Vatican II has not resolved and which continues to be debated. Among the sources given for canon 129§2 are important texts from Vatican II, more precisely *Lumen Gentium* n. 33 and *Apostolicam Actuositatem* n. 24. The former seems to imply that there are degrees of cooperaton possible, and the latter expounds how the apostolate of lay people has varying kinds of relationship with the hierarchy.

As for canon 135, we recall that this divides the power of governance into legislative, executive and judicial. It is probably in the nineteenth century that this threefold division of legislative, executive and judicial became widespread, although it had antecedents.

At Vatican II, and as so often in the context of episcopal authority, it was taught in *Lumen Gentium* n. 27 that the bishops (described as 'Vicars of Christ') govern also by authority and sacred power (*sacra potestas*).

> By virtue of this power, bishops have the sacred right and duty before the Lord of making laws for their subjects [*legislative*], of passing judgment on them [*judicial*], and of directing everything that concerns the ordering of worship and the apostolate [*executive*].

Albert Gauthier OP believed that *Lumen Gentium* n. 27 uses a vocabulary close to that used in the modern threefold analysis of authority in the state. To bring this out, I have inserted the three terms in brackets.

Because there is no single Book of the Code given over to it, one has to search throughout the 1983 Code for instances of this three-fold power of governance in the Church and where and how lay people can cooperate in its exercise. The most celebrated example is that a lay person can be a judge (canon 1421§2). More widely, canon 274§1 states that only clerics can obtain offices the exercise of which requires the power of order or ecclesiastical governance. This is broadly in line with what we have seen of canon 129. But we should complete the picture by referring to canon 228§1, which says that lay people who are found to be suitable are capable of being admitted by the sacred pastors to those ecclesiastical offices and functions which they can discharge.

The three canons, 129, 228 and 274, are not easy to align. We might say that only clerics can hold those offices that involve the power of governance, but that lay people can cooperate in the exercise of this power and also hold offices which do not involve it. Either way, there is a dependence by the laity on clerics in that the laity cooperate with what is essentially a clerical power (canons 129 and 274) or are given office by clerics (canon 228).

Specific issues

Since Vatican II there has been a great effort to place authority and governance in a wider, more inclusive, context and this has led to a re-evaluation of the contributions that can and should be made by the laity. There has also been much discussion about the appropri-ate use of 'democracy' within the Church, a concept with its com-plexities and its own long history. Perhaps 'participation' and 'collaboration' are better concepts than 'democracy' for use within the Church. These terms are more suited to express the dependence of all the faithful on *Christ's* salvific authority and their interdependence on one another.

'Authority' is an extremely wide term in a Christian context and all the baptized share in their own way Christ's threefold office of priest, prophet and king. This gives lay people great scope to exercise their gifts and abilities in and for the Church. The Books of the Code that deal with the teaching office and the sanctifying office contain several examples of what the laity can do: from preaching to acting as extraordinary ministers of Communion. It is the third dimension, the royal function of Christ, that is still proving hardest to apply.

To what extent can a lay person exercise in the Church authority in the sense of power of governance? In this final section, we can look at some examples in areas where history offers guidance and stimulus. The notion of 'subversive memory' is at play here, and tribute should be paid to Cardinal Yves Congar OP for all that he did to retrieve so much of our past so as to increase present understanding and offer guidance for the future. His book *Jalons pour une théologie du laicat* (Paris, 1953) is something of a milestone. It is partly because of Congar's researches that it is far less true to say now what he said in 1951; 'the laity's place in the Church's law is not so slight as some people allege, but it is little enough'.

Congar divided Part II of his pioneering book into chapters which examine the laity in terms of the Church's priestly, kingly and prophetical functions. This tripartite division was to enter Vatican II through Congar; it is, as we have seen, fundamental to the new canon law.

Lay people share Christ's office of king, and therefore they do have authority. Congar analysed the kind of 'royal' authority possessed by lay persons into, first, kingship over self and, second, kingship over the world. There is much to be said for using and developing these categories, given the contribution all the baptized are to make to the mission of the Church, to transforming the self and the world into God's kingdom. It was as part of his reflections on Vatican II's decree on the apostolate of the laity that Archbishop Worlock warned of the ever-present danger of the lay person's overinvolvement in 'churchy' things to the neglect of his or her mission in the secular world. He quoted Paul VI saying that the primary and immediate task of lay people is not to establish and develop the ecclesial community – this is the specific role of pastors.

To see the authority as service is of course to state one of its important, Christ-like characteristics. But to say that authority is service, which we should, does not answer the fundamental questions of *who* has authority and in *what* sense. It has been traditional to describe the Pope as 'servant of the servants'; clearly there are different ways to serve in the Church, there is a distribution of charisms and offices.

The five topics chosen by Congar for an historical examination would prove helpful and liberating in today's Church:

1 Election and provision to church offices.
2 The laity and councils.
3 Kings in the Church.
4 The life of the community.
5 The Church's executive power.

I agree with Congar that what has to be examined is the Church's tradition, expressed by actual facts at least as much as in doctrinal texts: Congar's discussion of them is still an excellent place from which to begin the conversation, which continues.

In conclusion I raise, *in a serene spirit*, some questions about the unfinished business set on the agenda by the 1983 Code. I choose these topics with an eye to the historical evidence marshalled by Congar and others.

IN WHAT PRACTICAL WAYS CAN WE FACILITATE LAY PARTICIPATION IN THE VARIOUS KINDS OF COUNCILS AND SYNODS OF THE CHURCH?

In England, as elsewhere, there was a tradition of holding diocesan synods, even after the Reformation, but although this tradition has been continued in various countries since Vatican II there seems to be no interest in it here. This is ironic. Synods are not in favour precisely now that canon law (canon 463) has restored the ancient practice of allowing the diocesan bishop to convoke lay people as synod members. A synod is an important moment in the life of a local church, a time of responsible decision-making and assessment of the state of the diocese. At it, the bishop can act as legislator, and the lay members present could make a formal, structured contribution to the legislative dimension of the power of governance.

Even apart from diocesan synods, there is much scope for lay participation in various diocesan and parish councils and finance committees. Canon 228§2 provides that suitable lay people are capable of being experts or advisers, even in councils, to assist pastors of the Church.

CAN THE INVOLVEMENT OF LAY PEOPLE IN THE CHOOSING OF BISHOPS AND PARISH PRIESTS BE IMPROVED?

The Pope freely appoints bishops or confirms those lawfully elected (canon 377). In the Latin Church there are extremely few examples left of dioceses retaining the right to elect their own bishop, but church history shows a wide variety of practices, and the matter cannot be said to be settled definitively. Quite apart from direct lay involvement in the choice of a bishop, and history contains abuses and mistakes as well as worthwhile models, it is the current law that the papal legate, if he judges it expedient, is also to seek individually, and in secret, the opinions of lay people of outstanding wisdom (canon 377).

Appointment to the office of parish priest belongs to the diocesan bishop, who is free to confer it on whomsoever he wishes, unless someone else has a right of presentation or election (canon 523). In conferring the office of parish priest, in order to assess suitability, the bishop is to conduct suitable enquiries and if appropriate seek the view of some lay people (canon 524).

ARE THERE SUFFICIENT LAY PEOPLE FILLING THE POSTS AND OFFICES OPEN TO THEM IN THE ROMAN CURIA AND AT DIOCESAN AND PARISH LEVEL?

This is a matter of maximizing the role of the God-given experience and expertise of the laity in the Church and of making the lay contribution visible and dignified.

There are numerous ways lay people enrich the life of the Church at all levels, often and perhaps generally without being structured into ministries or offices. This is how it should be. But the exercise of authority and governance is also structured, channelled and defined. For the first time, and no doubt in relation to secular developments in the area of human rights, there is something like a fundamental charter of rights in canons 208–23. This applies to all the faithful, and it is specified and modified for the laity by canons 224–31.

This is a vision in search of implementation, and in future we shall gradually find ways of giving scope to the rights of lay faithful. It cannot be done today, but by reading canons 208–31 one will soon have an agenda of proposals and suggestions bearing on the exercise of authority by lay people in the Church.

Conclusion

The matter of authority and governance in the Church is far from
settled. We do not possess a full understanding of the questions or
the answers, and we do not have a practice that is uniformly adequate even to such understanding as we have.

It would be difficult for a variety of reasons to survey historically
the authority held by lay persons in the Church. Much of the evidence would be contingent rather than structural in that, unlike
the clergy, 'the laity' has never been organized as one articulated
group, with defined internal structures and functions. At different
times and in different places some of the laity, in particular royalty
and the nobility, did have considerable authority over clerics and
over church property and affairs. This is why in Congar's celebrated
Jalons there is a separate section on 'kings in the Church'.

Not everything that has happened in history (especially in the
area of lay authority) establishes tradition in its correct theological
sense or should be repeated in different circumstances. There have
been abuses too. Any historical survey would have to examine
each of the great controversies over undue secular influence in
church matters. There are examples from all periods of church
history, the investiture controversy of the eleventh and twelfth centuries being the most famous of the examples up to the end of the
Middle Ages.

Given that ideas about authority in the Church will inevitably be
affected by secular politics and social realities, it may be worthwhile
to glance at the great controversies concerning lay authority over
clerics and church property and affairs since the Reformation in
the sixteenth century. In a Catholic context we should examine Gal-
licanism, Febronianism and Josephinism in Europe, and the 'trustees system' in the nineteenth-century United States. The presence
of so much conflict and polemic over lay authority in the Church
could be a sign of unsettled theological opinion, as well as being the
rejection of well-founded principles. Examination of modern controversies would show the difficulties inherent in adapting church
structures to modern political/constitutional expectations as well
as excessive and inappropriate demands. A letter written in 1815
by Fenwick, part of the debate over the 'trustees system' of the
United States, is revealing: 'What will you do with, or can you
expect from young harebrained Americans? . . . so infatuated with
the sound of liberty and equality.'

What are the implications of these modern constitutional crises in
society and in the Church after Vatican II and now that canon law

affirms a genuine equality of dignity and action among all Christ's faithful?

To move from history to doctrine, we should read the 1988 post-synodal exhortation *Christifideles Laici*, particularly nn. 22–3. Generally, this document understands lay ministries and offices as firmly related to and dependent on the ordained ministry. But to conclude, the *Catechism of the Catholic Church* offers in one page a summary of the kind of thinking I have been trying to unpack. The relevant page (paras 908–13) is headed 'Participation in Christ's Kingly Office'.

The first two paragraphs quote Vatican II and seem to echo Congar's presentation of the laity's kingship as being over self and over the world. The third paragraph quotes Paul VI saying that the laity can be called to cooperate with their pastors in the service of the ecclesial community. This can be done through the exercise of different kinds of ministries according to the grace and charisms bestowed by the Lord.

The fourth paragraph quotes canon 129§2 of the 1983 Code and gives specific examples drawn from canon law of what lay cooperation in the power of governance can mean. All the examples mentioned by the *Catechism* have already been referred to in this paper, except for the possibility that a lay person can share in the pastoral care of a parish. This last possibility (canon 517) could prove to be a striking new factor in church life. The last two paragraphs call on the faithful to distinguish and harmonize the rights and duties they have as Church members from those they have as members of human society. Finally, the *Catechism* affirms that each of the baptized is the witness and living instrument of the Church's mission.

References

The Canon Law: Letter and Spirit (1995), London: Geoffrey Chapman. (This includes a translation of the 1983 Code of Canon Law.)

Catechism of the Catholic Church (revised edition 1999), London: Geoffrey Chapman.

Congar, Yves (1959) *Lay People in the Church*, London: Bloomsbury.

Chapter Seven

A POLITICAL ECONOMY OF CATHOLICISM

Francis Davis

Francis Davis was educated by the Benedictines, at Durham University and the School of Oriental and African Studies, University of London. A former community worker and BBC Radio contributor, he founded and coordinated the Centre for Voluntary Sector Studies at La Sainte Union College of Higher Education (now Southampton University New College). He has undertaken consultancy with UK, East European, Asian and North American religious voluntary organizations and retains advisory and trustee roles with several European non-profits. Married with three young children, since 1998 he has been managing director of a leading century-old family enterprise in the design and print industry.

The problems uncovered in the attempt to establish frameworks for analysing the Church, its governance and notions of authority are legion. First, there is the political conflict over who should be concerned about authority and governance in any case. Second, there is the huge gap in the research literature of organizational psychology, decision-making studies, political science, management studies, and voluntary/third-sector studies when it comes to Christian organizations in general and the Catholic Church in particular. Third – and possibly most significantly – there is the question of epistemology. For example, in his pioneering study of global political Catholicism, Hanson (1995) comments that one of the difficulties faced by those seeking to analyse the Church by mobilizing the (modern) social sciences is that the Church – at least at the formal level – perceives itself to be inspired by a different set of norms, norms rooted in what we might term pre-modern frameworks of reflection.

A short chapter such as this then must acknowledge its limitations for the task of analysis. Particularly at a time when the Church in the

West faces such profound demographic changes, the main task is possibly more to find new ways to ask questions about governance and authority than to attempt to elucidate normative answers/ hopes about problems and opportunities.

Perhaps such an exercise is particularly important in the light of the contributions in the present collection, many of which seem to suggest the relevance of a voluntary-sector theory, organizational theory, or a clear vision of theology as a foundation for analysis of the Church. This chapter, the reflections of an activist in the Church's social apostolate, also draws on a number of interviews carried out with lay Catholic workers between 1989 and 1992. I want to suggest that it is the very assumption of clarity on the part of both conservatives and radicals which obscures from our view a number of key issues in relation to governance and authority. These issues, which can only be introduced here, fall roughly into three areas: What is our dominant image of the Church? What do we know about how decisions are made? Who are the key players in the Church's decision-making and leadership? Throughout I will be particularly concerned about issues relating to the allocation of the Church's material resources, partly because the Church in Britain seems occasionally to underestimate its material impact. Recent US 'economic impact' studies of church organizations have surprised their authors by the scope of activity they have uncovered, and the Church in Britain is surely not insignificant, especially in its relative strongholds. Moreover, it is not unreasonable to suggest that exhortation to mission without an allocation of proportional resources is often a sign of lack of missionary commitment.

What is our Dominant Image of the Church?

Gareth Morgan (1986) has argued that the way we think about organizations can go a long way to explaining how we actually run them. While most of us would deny any great intellectual, theological or organizational insight, each of us actually thinks quite hard about our image of the Church, whether we work in bishops' conferences or feel part of the put-upon 'poor bloody infantry' at parochial level.

In this section I want to suggest that one of the dominant images, or metaphors, that we have constructed for the Church in England and Wales is similar to the 'community of service' ideal found in Beyer and Nutzinger's (1993) research on employment patterns in German church institutions. Subsequently, I want to examine the validity, and usefulness, of this image in helping the Church's decision-makers fully to understand the organizational realities of the Church today.

On the basis of a survey of a range of staff in Christian welfare organizations, Beyer and Nutzinger identify a pattern of beliefs suggesting that as far as the Christian community, and especially its leadership, go, there is a normative sense of purpose overarching the activities of all church institutions – both worshipping communities and non-worshipping communities. Taken together the activities of all church institutions could be descriptively distilled as a community of service.

> Community of service means that all parties in church institutions are members of a community with a special mission based on fundamental principles ... where the normative concept is that all (workers) agree that their individual work is also part of the service of the lord.
>
> (Beyer and Nutzinger, 1993)

In this study the implications of the community of service ideal are extensive. For example, at times of tension over salaries between employed staff in church institutions an appeal was made to the community of service idea by the Church leadership. Despite what staff interviewed saw as a clash between labour and capital within the Church community/institution, and notwithstanding the presence of non-professing staff in the organizations surveyed, all were alleged to be on the same side despite their different perspectives. Everyone was said to share an overarching commitment to 'the service of the lord' and hence to 'the community of service'.

Arguably, in England and Wales something akin to the community of service ideal/image provides a related but different effect. The community of service ideal serves an image of the Church which suggests that the purposes and practices of the Church are commonly agreed and that although there may be different perspectives on, for example, the ordination of women, the relationship of the Church to capitalism or – my main concern – disagreement over how material resources should be allocated, the opposing extremes in such debates are not identified as mutually exclusive but part of the ebb and flow of relationships in one unified whole organization often described as 'the body of Christ' or 'the family of the Church'. For example the vicar general of one English diocese argued in his 1996 Christmas newsletter that 'right wing, left wing, centrist or radical we are all one Church ... and there is room for all of us in the family of the Church'. This image of the community of service is reinforced by notions such as 'collegiality' and

'collaborative ministry' and the seeming increase in interest in consensus. We are all members of one body because we are all 'equal'
and 'baptized'. In this sense, often repeated today, 'we are all
Church' not only on Sunday but throughout the week.

In the light of the Second Vatican Council, some might argue,
such an image of the Church is unsurprising and, in fact, inspiring.
The question we need to ask, however, is to what extent this image
of a community of service or of being one body relates to the empirical policy practice of the Church.

Our 'one Church' in Britain is made up of three bishops' conferences who, between them, have pastoral responsibility in four
nations. In England and Wales there are 24 dioceses which, despite
bishops' conferences, are the pastoral groupings to which the Holy
See relates. Each of these dioceses, while served by bishops who
share, theologically speaking, in the pastoral work of the papacy, is
divided into deaneries and parishes which are in turn served by
priests who pastor in the bishop's stead. In passing, we should note
that other parts of this 'one Church' include a range of religious
orders whose governing constitutions vary in character from the
Dominican to the Jesuit, a substantial number of official agencies
at the diocesan and bishops' conference levels, and a vast array of
identifiably Catholic organizations that are not official agencies
but which compete for material resources. This is without mention-
ing our private schools, which continue to be objects of Catholic phi-
lanthropy, and our state schools, which comprise 10 per cent of
public sector education provision. Moreover, if all that the baptized
do is a feature of the Church, the Church is also, for example, an MP
in London, a beggar in Farnham, a businessman in Glasgow, a
shopkeeper in Preston and a cleaner in Hammersmith. And, if we
take natural law (or liberation theology for that matter) seriously,
the Church extends at least a sense of sharing in the project to 'all
people of good will' or 'the poor' whether they know (or like) it or
not.

At the national level the following imaginary extended case based
on a number of real organizations may ring bells for those who have
ever tried to run a Catholic organization in recent years:

> Catholic HIV/AIDS Action is – we may imagine – a national
> charity founded some years ago. Its annual income is £550,000,
> partly garnered from the Department of Health but mostly
> raised via the Church. It employs a director, a trainer and three
> secretaries in its central office in London as well as supporting a
> network of volunteers. It is not an official agency of its bishops'

conference. Three bishops have barred the organization from their dioceses because the organization provides its services 'non-judgementally' – a term which is seen as supporting homosexual lifestyles – but almost unbeknown to those local ordinaries, the organization does run seven projects in the three geographical areas of those dioceses as part of its response to Department of Health grant criteria of providing a 'national service'.

In 2001 a major piece of legislation is proposed in the form of a White Paper by the government which will lead to an effective withdrawal of NHS-funded care for those dying of an AIDS-related condition if they cannot prove that they contracted the virus from non-sexual activity.

The day after the publication of the White Paper the phone is ringing non-stop because the media, looking for a Catholic angle, have tracked down HIV/AIDS Action. Most diocesan press officers have also referred enquirers on to the organization because they feel embarrassed to comment. Halfway through her twelfth interview, the director is told that the bishops' conference is on the line and needs a briefing on how on earth to respond as they have no staff member with expertise in the HIV area. They also tell the director that about 20 secular organizations who are shocked by the White Paper have phoned in asking for Catholic support. The bishops' conference start referring all organizational, press and individual enquiries to HIV/AIDS Action. Soon HIV/AIDS Action – the representative of 'one Church' – is part of a coalition of groups campaigning against the Bill which will implement the White Paper's proposals. The organization's line is that cutting such care is disgraceful because all who are sick deserve love and support: HIV/AIDS Action is attacked by a conservative Catholic newspaper for affirming the homosexual lobby and castigated by part of the Church's justice and peace movement for not affirming gay lifestyles more aggressively. Meanwhile, the archbishop who chairs the bishops' conference begins to realize that the Bill, though presenting difficulties, actually presents a clear opportunity for the Church to be seen as caring for homosexual people without affirming their lifestyles at the same time. In trying to prepare his press releases and articles in *The Times*, not to mention a statement that he wants the bishops' conference to make, he requests that the Director of HIV/AIDS Action should attend each and every one of his pre-paration meetings as the Church's expert in this field. Sucked into this and feeling that the organization cannot let the Church down and knowing that the bishops control access to fundraising

for the organization, the director of HIV/AIDS Action helps out
and the number of days away from the office start ratcheting up.
This director cannot call on the research departments of secular
agencies or their public relations departments because, unlike
them, she does not have 20-plus staff.

Before long the organization's service delivery is struggling,
and its Department of Health grant being questioned: the organization is now rudderless as the director and the secretaries try to
meet the demands placed on them by the bishops' conference,
the dioceses, the archbishop's office, the Catholic right, the
Catholic left, other church groups, as well as the wider lobbying
coalition against the Bill and the organization's clients. The
director does suggest a small grant from the bishops' conference
to buy in a general manager for six months, but this is met
with warm smiles and the assertion that 'we are all part of the
Church'.

Although this example is imaginary, the tensions will be clear and
find their parallels in the stresses on a parish priest criticized by parishioners for being away too often as chair of the diocesan schools
commission, or an inner-city deanery youth worker who loses part
of his trust funding because of being continually called upon by the
diocesan youth office to 'help out' elsewhere in the diocese, or even
in an official overseas aid body of a bishops' conference which has
to cover up for the extremely poor development work of another
Catholic charity in order to safeguard its own reputation, and the
reputation of the Church, for the future. In addition, we might
mention the bishop who was asked recently how many staff his
diocese employed. His response of 'twelve' recognized his Curial
employees but failed to appreciate that his central offset banking
system, into which all parishes contract, makes him/the diocese in
civil law legally responsible for over 100 staff employed by parishes.

The point is that while we might talk and think all the time within
the frameworks of collegiality, one Church, community of service
and increasingly collaborative ministry, this dominant image/me-
taphor actually obscures from our view both the intense competition that has grown up in Catholic networks for resources and
attention and the profound confusion of how the Church should
decide, preach and act. The reality is probably closer to a view that
suggests that the Catholic world is made up of hundreds of organizations and images of the Church in intense conflict – and some of
them mutually exclusive in orientation – rather than of some
clearly shared project/normative metaphor. It is conceivable that

in turn these images of Church are actually rooted in different theories about life and notions of God.

To learn then about how decisions are made in the Church, and particularly about the allocation of material resources, we need to learn more about which images of Church and life are truly in play at any given decision-making moment. This is not necessarily an argument for rejecting the community of service ideal but more an argument for taking a long, reflective look at the 'is' of Church decision-making rather than the 'ought', a distinction which theologizing often confuses.

What do we Know about How Decisions are Made?

In recent years a great deal of research has been focused on the nature of decision-making, particularly among what are termed 'policy elites' (e.g. Migdal, 1988; Migdal et al., 1994). There is an emerging research consensus that, despite structural factors, decision-makers still have and can create 'policy space' in which to manoeuvre. From their research Grindle and Thomas (1991) identify certain factors that influence the nature of decisions taken by decision-makers from within those policy spaces. These include personal attributes and goals, ideological predispositions, professional expertise and training, memories of similar policy experiences, position and power resources, and political and institutional commitments and loyalties. The purpose of identifying such factors is twofold: first it helps us understand the cause of certain policy choices. Second, it also enables us in some instances to recognize factors that may be involved in decision-making that are actually unrelated to the putative rationality of choices made. For example, infinite demands may be made by a number of groups, often with incommensurable aims, seeking what are termed 'rents' (e.g. government funding) on the state apparatus. If these are granted – particularly if this happens by 'non-rational' processes (i.e. allocation on the grounds of kinship or political expediency) – then a number of consequences may follow. Policy may change, core policy priorities become unimplementable because key resources are diverted or lost, and – despite mighty flown rhetoric – the state apparatus may actually begin to fracture and decay as its resources are scattered in a thousand disparate directions. For those concerned with public management then there is a vital task to accelerate the competence/rationality of decision-making at every level of the state bureaucracy.

Given this perspective on the nature of decision-making in state

institutions one might subsequently ask whether, for all the implementing force that the Curia can summon with regard to certain
cases, the main decision-maker in the Church – the ordained celi-
bate male cleric, whether parish priest, provincial, bishop or cardinal – actually has considerable scope for manoeuvre? Either way
what are the forces at play in the way that he allocates clergy, staff,
real estate and financial resources within, across and possibly
beyond the Catholic community? Is the cleric as decision-maker in-
sulated from the rent-seeking forces of particular causes and crusades or does he feel constricted by the need to placate certain
forces within the Catholic community to maintain peace, square
his relations with another part of the Church, or simply to maintain
popularity (legitimacy?) in the eyes of his parishioners and possibly
– perhaps more importantly – his brother clerics? Is his dominant
image of the Church 'the community of service' and if so does he
feel he has to provide a little bit to everyone or does he feel able to
identify key priorities, such as an option for the poor, and drive
them forward with more targeted resources? For example, the
policy choices (let us call them pastoral priorities) of an archbishop
in a Vatican department of state may be determined by any
number of the factors outlined by Grindle and Thomas and this
may run on down through any layer of the clerical machine. Is the
priest/bishop a risk-taker, happy with conflict, or simply convinced
that if he prays the decision will be shown to him (personal attributes)? Is he steeped in Oscar Romero's sermons or inspired by the
charismatic movement (ideological predispositions)? Was he an
accountant in an international company before ordination and
trained at the Beda or did he go to junior seminary from the age of
11, 12 miles from his home town, and never travel overseas (professional expertise and training)? Does he respond in different ways
to similar problems as they emerge or is his habitual response due
to the fact that it worked for his bishop when he was a bishop's
secretary 24 years ago (previous experience)? Is his diocese, his
religious order, or his department large or small, or does he still
go walking each Wednesday with Cardinal Ratzinger who taught
him theology at university (position, access and power resources)?
Does he welcome the YCW to his diocese because the local cardinal
is a great fan or does he support the Neo-Catechumenate because
without their mobilization of foreign financial support the diocese
would go bust (political and institutional commitments and
loyalties)?

And what does that clerical decision-maker believe he is doing?
For example, imagine if one was a pope who allocated huge

resources to Solidarity, unstintingly lobbied G7 leaders in defence of Poland's cause, but after Solidarity's victory attributed the whole thing not to one's own efforts or policy choices but to 'Our Lady drawing her veil over Poland'. Or does such a pope speak with the formal ideological expressions of Vatican II but actually respond from within profoundly pre-Vatican II informal ideological paradigms because of generation, geography of training, and life experience? For example, using almost religious language, Levine (1994) has suggested that even post-revolutionary elites in China, although trained in academies with formal Party approval, still respond from informal ideological frameworks because of their pre-revolutionary formation in the great tales and histories of China as the centre of global affairs and moral governance.

This process of identifying why certain choices are being made would be one first step to clarifying the matching of resources (or not) to professed mission priorities and practice. It would certainly make things more transparent and hopefully eliminate a variety of poor decisions which may sometimes be made. It might hold in check the glorification found in some circles of chaos and poor stewardship as 'the mess of human life and incarnation'. It could possibly increase income in the long term by encouraging a more widespread sense of the ownership of giving and it might contribute at the least to a ring-fencing of resources of time and money to encourage work focus. Vitally it might also lead to the discovery that a diocese, for example, has developed such a broad definition of the community of service (or another image) that competing voices and images of the Church are actually reproducing a form of extreme rent-seeking on endowments, congregations and investments. This may in turn demonstrate that a public commitment to a particular form of mission cannot be moved forward in anything but words because of the inertia caused by mission distortion, weight of spending on alternative and opposing ministries, and dissipation of energy as volunteers and clergy are distributed in every conceivable direction at parish and diocesan level. Given such institutional dissipation it would be unsurprising if priests often felt pulled in all directions.

By way of symbolic contrast, we may note the proposal during 1989/90 in the Portsmouth Anglican Diocese that the parochial poll tax to the central diocesan body should be levied not on the number of congregation members but on the basis of the extent of poverty identified (by national poverty statistics) in the local parochial area. This would have the effect of affirming the real struggles of the poor of the diocese, of maintaining resources in poor economic areas which were experiencing too much capital flight anyway, releasing resources in poor areas for social ministry, and encouraging richer areas to improve their fundraising techniques to meet their new responsibilities to the diocese and – by implication – to the poor.

It may be objected at this point that my emphasis on individual (clerical) decision-makers is elitist, too narrow, and does not adequately address the emergence of collaborative ministry and consensus-building as the basis for decision-making. I shall address this point a little more fully in the next section, but I want here to stress that consensus, in Christian terms, may be valid but, if we take formal Catholic teaching seriously, only if it is metaphysical rather than political. By this I mean that it is an insight of modern political science that justice in liberal societies has become what we can instrumentally agree on as a polity at any one time rather than being a value in its own right and in relation to some underpinning notion of telos (Rawls, 1972). Given that Catholics in England and Wales are more profoundly schooled in modernism today – particularly when encouraged to 'reflect on their own experience' – than in the virtues, there is a danger that consensus-building in what we might term the polity of the Church becomes the thinnest point of agreement between all the competing images that Catholic organizations and individuals proclaim about the Church. By its nature then this is a 'thin' political subjective consensus rather than a rich, or 'thick' objective articulation of Catholic insights. Thus in some instances while a consensus may have been achieved in the name of God it may actually be closer in reality to some form of political accommodation between competing voices seeking resources of dominance for their image of the organization of the Church. This may temporarily overcome an institutional legitimation crisis, but it tends again to organizational inertia and fracture in the longer term. So, if consensus is the preferred model for decision-making we will still need to hear why and discover more about how a theological consensus may or may not be merely a political accommodation rather than the discovery of a deeper metaphysical reality formed around a common conception of the telos of the Church.

But this relates directly of course to who makes decisions and how they come to be in those positions of influence over the Church's material resources in the first place. It is that to which I now turn.

Who are the Key Players in the Church's Decision-Making and Leadership?

It is rarely acknowledged that most secular priests come forward from their own diocesan geographical areas to have their own training funded by their own diocese to which they will return to be 'incardinated' on a permanent basis (i.e. for life) and to serve – theoretically – in whichever parishes the bishop places them. Even in past periods of comparatively high clerical vocations dioceses would then be drawing for their leadership on a comparatively restricted pool of mostly local men who, once ordained, would remain the pool of personnel upon which the diocese could call given any number of changes in the external or internal environment. Even in days gone past, the matching of skills or merit to the practical tasks required, and the allocation of material resources, was never a clear option because bishops could only really choose those who were members of the ordained priesthood in that diocese. There has never been a necessary relationship between competence in the range of skills needed, beyond the act of consecration, and the allocation of clerical resources. Consequently, it has been ordination and not necessarily skill/competence which provided the primary ground upon which clergy are released/permitted to work in certain parishes.

With the decline in vocations this limited pool of localized talent has been even further restricted, and arguably some dioceses are now reproducing some of the more acute problems faced by the most unlucky kinds of third- or fourth-generation family businesses. So we may therefore experience first of all a shortage of 'talent in the family' upon which to draw for staffing in general and to take up senior positions at a later stage. Second, 'older members of the family' have to forego retirement to sustain the enterprise, and this in turn reduces the organization's openness to change. Lastly, there is a danger of rapidly reducing quality in decision-making not from lack of commitment and willingness, but from lack of appropriate competence.

Such problems are important to note because one response to deceleration in the availability of clerical human resources has been the development of lay ministries in general and talk of collaborative ministry in particular. This allegedly involves discovering new models of Church that enable priests and people to work together to share their common rootedness in baptism. Ordained priesthood here is often talked of as 'different' not 'superior' (although I still ponder on the claim of the seminarian who told me a few years ago that he would be 'ontologically superior' to a lay person after ordination, and some Vatican texts still talk of the 'objective superiority' of the ordained man). There is a hope in the language of collaborative ministry that the equality that accrues to us all in baptism will become the ground of a new set of relationships where priests and people work together in a way that perhaps they did not in pre-conciliar days. In terms of those who makes decisions about the Church's material resources is this really convincing and satisfactory as a reality rather than a theological 'ought to be'?

First, it is not unfair to suggest that the cleric is present in the relationship of collaboration not necessarily because of skills he has but simply because he is a priest. To use the family business analogy, it is a little like saying that son X has much to contribute to this set of decisions not because he may or may not be up to the task but because he is a member of the family. Second, it is important to ask where the lay people come from who are in collaboration with the priest in, say, a parish. If it is an area of very low social mobility with an ageing demographic profile, or in a rich commuter area where only a tiny proportion of people live for more than six months at a time, the lay component of the relationship may itself reproduce aspects of the family business insularity. And if the lay people encouraged to join a finance committee or any other pastoral grouping are encouraged to do so by the priest, to what extent is the priest, or other lay people, competent to judge whether decisions would be better made in a Church setting with advice from the finance director of BAT, a professor of accounting, or a local charity's bookkeeper, all of whom might be found in his parish and each with different images of what makes an organization tick financially/mission-wise. Will the best decision-makers really always be found in one parish, or diocese, and once identified do they need to be used in broader ways that transcend traditional boundaries? Lastly, when it comes to material decision-making the relationship of lay people is, according to canon law, only advisory to the priest. In the end, and no matter what his possible lack of competence in any given field, he can reject it all as can the Curial offices (and the bishop as key trustee) in a central offset system. How truly collaborative is that?

Conclusion

In this chapter I asked whether the dominant images that we have constructed to describe the organizational reality of the Church are adequate to the task. I suggested that underneath the seemingly normative and straightforward claims of those who might, for example, be called conservatives, liberals and radicals has arisen an incommensurable number of images of the Church which are now in intense conflict and competition. Drawing on recent research on decision-makers I subsequently suggested that the danger of this confusion of images was that it might accelerate institutional fracture, mission distortion and inertia while at the same time giving the impression of great activity and expansive commitment. This is because each articulation of image is more often than not matched with a separate claim for material resources. Lastly I have wondered whether in the Church we have confused individual competence or skill to make decisions with an individual's alleged theological status, and geographical presence. Does this mean that at many levels of the Church ordination, local knowledge, orthodoxy, reputation, perceived holiness or marital status – political acceptability – have become the key to being promoted as a good decision-maker? And has this been achieved at the expense of competence in governance – or merit – and a decline in real authority?

None of the foregoing is meant as a criticism of either bishops, priests, or lay people or of collaborative ministry. It is intended to suggest that unlike secular voluntary organizations or public and private bodies which can cast their net ever wider in search of the right skills, talent, resources and competences Catholic organizations are more restricted than they think by the intense localism of Catholicism, declining resources, and the specificity of perceived core beliefs. This comes just at the time when the number of images of the Church seems to be increasing, not to mention demands from both the previous Conservative government and the current New Labour one that, 'the Church should do more'.

The lack of reflection on such limitations in the face of huge demands risks scarce resources being dissipated in pursuit of too many tasks and via possibly less-than-competent policy-making bodies/individuals just at the moment when we need to be clearer about our role, more certain of our potential and more focused in elucidating and implementing our vision of the future. Do we need to do less more effectively? We certainly need to reflect on such questions more deeply.

A more focused approach need not be managerialist but could be what other organizations would call having a credible strategic plan at each appropriate level. Perhaps our task should be to match clear vision to coherent, researched and planned decisions about training of our people and allocation of our financial resources through the waste of which we become legends in our own minds – collapsing slowly while protesting our universal potential and uniqueness?

Francis Davis

References

Beyer, H. and Nutzinger, H. (1993) 'Hierarchy or Co-operation: Labour Management Relations in Church Institutions', *Voluntas* 4(1).

Grindle, M. and Thomas, J. (1991) *Public Choices and Policy Change*, Baltimore and London: Johns Hopkins University Press.

Hanson, E. (1995) *The Catholic Church in World Politics*, Princeton: Princeton University Press.

Levine, S. (1994) in Robinson, M. and Shambaugh, D. (eds), *Chinese Foreign Policy*, Oxford: Clarendon.

Migdal, J. (1988) *Strong Societies and Weak States*, Princeton: Princeton University Press.

Migdal, J., Kohli, A and Shue, V. (eds) (1994) *State Power and Social Forces*, Cambridge: Cambridge University Press.

Morgan, G. (1986) *Images of Organisation*, London: Sage.

Rawls, J. (1972) 'Justice as Fairness: Political not Metaphysical', *Philosophy and Public Affairs* 14(3).

Rueschmeyer, D. and Skocpol, T. (eds) (1985) *Bringing the State Back In*, Cambridge: Cambridge University Press.

Chapter Eight

A THEOLOGY OF GOVERNANCE: GOD AND THE CHURCH

Enda McDonagh

Enda McDonagh is a priest of the Archdiocese of Tuam, Ireland. He was Professor of Moral Theology at the Pontifical University, Maynooth, 1960–95, and has been visiting professor and lecturer at universities in the UK, USA, Europe, Australia and Africa. He is a member of Caritas International Task Force on HIV/AIDS, and was president of the National Conference of Priests of Ireland, 1995–8. He is the author and editor of 23 books on theological issues, and now working on *The Risk of God*. He is currently chair of the Governing Body of University College, Cork.

Language, Image and Concept

The many ways in which we speak of church and church governance have their roots in the Bible, particularly in the New Testament. However, subsequent history has added immensely to the complexity and resulting ambiguity which the pastoral inclusiveness and theological power of Vatican II could not wholly dissipate. If we are to be faithful to the tradition and authentically contemporary in our discussions we therefore have to accept the limitations and possibilities of plurality and ambiguity.

The Primacy and the Ultimacy of God

The presupposition of any discussion about God or of everything else in relation to God is that the final point of reference lies in the God of Jesus Christ. A theology of the Church or of church governance must therefore be presented on the understanding that it will eventually be open to and judged by the presence and character of God as manifest in Jesus Christ.

117

The Priority of the Believing People

Prior to 1964 the prevailing church order was perceived in terms of hierarchy and clergy with people attached. In 1964 *Lumen Gentium* reversed this, presenting in its place a people with an internal hierarchical structure. Such reversal nevertheless did little to affect the image (or reality) of one Church for the baptized and another for the ordained. The document itself is somewhat unclear, reflecting as it does divisions among the council fathers. Inevitable ambiguity therefore allows for conflicting interpretations which readily translate into power-struggles, accusations of bad faith or, at the very least, allegations of a mistaken reading of Vatican II.

Experience of Church

Plurality and ambiguity are nowhere more rampant than in historical or contemporary church experience, and this applies to particular groups: bishops, priests, lay people and different stages of life. Although we may each feel able to make coherent generalizations, the reality is that most of us experience different aspects of Church at different stages of our lives. To complicate matters further there may be real disagreement among us as to what actually qualifies as 'Church'. It was and is quite common for individuals who have been hurt by a particular priest or bishop to be told that the cleric concerned should not be confused with 'the Church'. Thus they are given to understand that their experience of hurt was not an experience of church. A somewhat similar statement asserts that while the Church is composed of sinners it is not itself sinful. It is important to stress the distinction between what might be described as the Church of empirical experience and the Church of faith idealization (the sinless Church) and the obligation of individuals and groups to share their experience of church.

Pilgrims in Communion

Two models of church are currently influential and helpful in illuminating personal experience of church and issues of governance. These are: the Church as pilgrim people and the Church as communion. In a classic study, Victor Turner suggests that the pilgrim people is a dynamic open group moving towards a future still largely unknown: movement rather than order, equality and mutuality in comradeship rather than status and superiority/inferiority. The pilgrim people function in response to needs rather than from set offices. The Church as communion suggests at first sight a more ordered and static group with overtones of hierarchy and exclusion. There are perceived associations between the understanding of the Church as communion and the perception of the Eucharist as the 'province' of a presiding superior with powers of exclusion. There are ambiguities in both models, such as the fact that pilgrim peoples readily develop hierarchy and exclusivity among themselves.

At a deeper theological level and in practical terms both pilgrimage and communion have much to offer in terms of experiencing and understanding the concept of governance in the Church. This is particularly significant where pilgrimage is seen as characteristic of humanity as well as of church, and it is essential that the Church should manifest and realize the concept of pilgrimage in its life and structures. There is, however, a tendency for the pilgrim people to seek refuge from reality in an apparently fixed order as a result of laziness or insecurity. Thus the dynamism, the equality and mutuality and the response to need require constant renewal. At another extreme the group may become chaotic. To continue on their pilgrim way, they need to be organized and sustained by thoughtful caring, and closer bonds of community need to be created. Thus the deeper reality of communion is both possible and provisional and always contains risk. In theological terms communion is the eschatological form of historical community. It is already and not yet, the heavenly dimension of the earthly Church partially realized. The Eastern and Western emphases in the understanding of church and eucharist are implicit here (expressed together in the common phrase 'communion of saints'). It is the expression in time of the eternal communion of the Trinity, in itself of course constituted by the dynamic and mutual loving of the three different but equally divine persons. Pilgrimage and communion then belong together as reinforcing yet mutually correcting models. The renewal of life and mutuality in what can be a juridicized static and oppressive community/communion model requires a more explicit realization of the pilgrim model. This might be helped for example by deliberate 'pilgrim Sundays' in parishes and dioceses where all status and privileges are set aside and people come together dressed only in their 'baptismal garments' as equal members of the pilgrim people with equal concern and responsibility for charting the course ahead.

The Church, Local and Global, Particular and Universal

The model of pilgrim people and the model of communion (as well as other models of church) have to take account of the peculiar

unity in diversity which characterizes the Church and its governance. The concept is more complex than the simple model of 'local'
and 'universal' might suggest. It has to take into account past and
future churches as well as forms of church which are not simply geographical, for example the traditional domestic church of the
family or the new informal 'basic Christian community'. In preparing for the future the interaction of past and present is critical to
the pilgrim model. In contemporary terms the concept of communion appears to give priority to the local and the global. In historical
and eschatalogical terms, however, the emphasis is placed upon the
tension between past, present and future. In any discussion on governance the voice of the past must be carefully heeded, but so too
must the voice of the present as the pilgrim people faces into the
next phase of the journey and seeks to discern and express communion among themselves at so many different levels.

Civil Structures, Church Governance and the Reign of God

The believing community strove first of all to follow the practice and
teaching of Jesus as expressed in the apostolic witness of the New
Testament. It involved, first, fellowship with the excluded and new
understanding of leadership which meant not lording like the Gen-
tiles, not acting as the scribes and Pharisees – saying but not doing.
Second, the believing community sought to respond to the needs of
the people under the guidance of the Holy Spirit. This involved the
emergence of diverse ministries in the New Testament churches
and their solidification into bishops, presbyters and deacons during
the second and third centuries with the gradual emergence of the association of the Petrine primacy with the see of Rome. Third, the believing community interacted with contemporary 'secular' civil
insights, structures and practices. This became more obvious with
the emergence of the churches from the catacombs into the basilicas
and the subsequent responsibility which church leaders had to
assume for peace and order in the wider society. Monarch-like
bishops and popes were the ambiguous fruits of these developments
in ways which are still quite influential.

It is easy to exaggerate the mistakes, some of which were in any
case inevitable. We need, however, to stress the necessity and appro-
priateness of the Church learning from and adapting governing
structures and practices of a particular time. Both Scripture and
history indicate that the *koinonia* or new community initiated by
Jesus did not contain a clear and complete blueprint for the
Church to come. One cannot move in a direct line from the

Gospels to the Code of Canon Law or even to *Lumen Gentium.* In following the Spirit the Church borrowed (somewhat uncritically perhaps) what it considered to be useful in the governing and organizing structures of the wider society. Just as the Church adopted the natural law as a basis for personal and social morality, including the morality of civil governance, so it could integrate elements of that sort of governance into its own life as witnessed by the development of canon law. And this could be justified theologically from the doctrine of creation and the doctrine of the reign of God, which was the leading edge of Jesus' teaching and mission. The new community was to proclaim and promote the reign of God which had already been initiated and was yet to be completed. The Church is at once the sign or sacrament as well as the proclaimer and promoter of the reign or presence of God in power, creating, sustaining, healing and transforming the universe, God's creation. Given the scope of this mission it is clear that it cannot be initiated or fulfilled within the Church alone. The Church is to discern and serve the coming of that kingdom or reign of God, and the kingdom is coming in ways and areas beyond its limits. One example is the healing dimension of the reign of God which cannot be confined to church even though the Church played and can still play an honourable role within the medical profession.

Fresh insight into and respect for the dignity of the human being with the accompanying recognition of certain inalienable human rights, including the right to participation in social governance, have yet to be realized properly and fully in our societies. Yet their development, however incomplete and even ambiguous, can be seen as *indicia regni Dei,* signs of the inbreaking reign of God. Should they not therefore play their due part in governance of the Church? Is this not all the more true if the Church is to be discerner and exemplar (sacrament) of God's reign as well as sacrament of the community of the whole human race (Vatican II)?

Further insight may be gained into the social and organizational dignity of the human being from the best management theories and practices, where these are concerned to promote human dignity and freedom. As such they can reveal something, albeit limited, of the emerging kingdom of God and can be appropriately integrated into the structures of the Church. Participation and subsidiarity are already part of the moral vocabulary of the Church and should as such play their part in good labour relations and the efficient use of resources in Church organization.It is also desirable that the Church should develop management skills and practices which are respectful of the human dignity of all its members and appropriate to its mission of promoting the reign of God.

The Rhetoric of Service and the Harsh Reality of Serving

Managerial skills for all their value cannot replace the true Christian understanding and practice of governance as a ministry or service, and there is a persistent danger of the rhetoric of service replacing the harsh reality of serving. While it is still very difficult for lay people to recognize in the privileges and practices of priests, bishops and pope their proclaimed status as servants, it is similarly hard for these clergy themselves to escape anti-Christian delusions of office which they have inherited. Church leaders are not alone in experiencing this problem. Political ministers, presidents and bureaucrats are equally prone to delusions of power and grandeur at the expense of service. It was to leaders of the believing community that the warning about 'lording it' was issued, however, and such behaviour is a double betrayal of the Church of Jesus Christ and of the human community. The better civil systems have developed corrective processes such as constitutions and laws to which all are equally subject. Leaders are thus accountable to their people through parliament, the media and the courts, and regular elections. While all is not perfect or even healthy in our democratic civil systems, they have adopted practices which the believing community should consider and even endorse for the health of its own internal life and the effectiveness of its kingdom mission.

The Recurring Risk of God

The phrase 'In the beginning God and in the end God' describes the outreach of the Christian community and sets the agenda for the discussion of reform in the field of church governance. The difficulty lies in discerning the route along which the Spirit of God is leading. Recognition of God as incomprehensible mystery and as Lord of history requires endless humility. The lessons of history suggest a God of surprises: the greatest surprise of all being God's initiative in giving us Jesus. At the heart of that surprise lies Calvary. The risks taken by God in creation and redemption are finally revealed. The response demanded of the believing community involves considerable risk, yet we will not be tested beyond our strength or God's strength in us and it is in a spirit of hope that we face the prospect of the renewal of Church governance.

Chapter Nine

AUTHORITY AS SERVICE IN COMMUNION

David McLoughlin

David McLoughlin is a priest of the Roman Catholic Archdiocese of Birmingham. He is Vice-President of the Catholic Theological Association of Great Britain and a member of the Bishops' Conference Theology Committee. He has worked for nearly 20 years with Christian worker movements in Britain and Europe, trying to develop praxis-based theology. He teaches theology to those preparing for ministry and organizes in-service courses for clergy, teachers and Christian activists. He is currently researching the theology of ministry, writing on models of hope and developing a theological reflection on work in a postmodern and late industrial context. At present he is Chaplain and Lecturer at Newman College, Birmingham, and a guest lecturer at Birmingham University.

The original meaning of 'ministry' relates to an activity of service: 'serving or responding to God's grace, serving people, serving God in the midst of his people' (Käsemann, 1968).

This chapter, which focuses on ministry, begins with a thumbnail sketch of ministry in the early Church as a backdrop to a discussion of the changing theology of episcopacy in the years following the Second Vatican Council.

Ministry in the Early Church

THE APOSTOLIC AGE (*c.* AD 27–70)

This period saw an extraordinary variety of ministry as the Church gradually distinguished itself from mainline Judaism. Ministry was regarded as a function common to many. If you read 1 Corinthians 12.4–11; Romans 12.6–8; Ephesians 4.11–16, you will find preaching, instruction, healing, miracle-working, prophecy, discernment, interpretation of tongues, teaching, exhortation, almsgiving, etc. –

all of which were seen as necessary to the building up of the community. From the beginning this variety of service was open to all the baptized whoever they were. Women, perhaps surprisingly, were key figures in the early communities. In Philippi and Derbe, for example, we hear of Lydia and Prisca (Acts 16; 2 Timothy 4). Widows and deaconesses were powerful figures, and even slaves who had been in trouble like Onesimus were included.

THE POST-APOSTOLIC AGE (AD 70–110)

The Jerusalem temple has gone, and Christians have been excluded from the synagogue. Priests as we understand the term have not yet emerged, instead the whole community is called priestly. The vision of ministry varies as the different communities deal with their different contexts. Matthew's community emphasizes the passing on of solid teaching and the role of recognized leaders like Peter, over and above the more charismatic prophets. John's community was more egalitarian, emphasizing closeness to the Lord in love, with no special emphasis on the role of the twelve apostles.

In general, ministry implies action and service, a response to a call and a gift for building up the body. A call and gift which the community cheerfully recognized for it was not a power or honour to be possessed.

PERIOD OF ESTABLISHMENT (AD 110–313)

According to Paul Bernier (1992, p. 58) this period marks the extraordinary spread of Christian communities throughout the Roman empire, stimulated often by persecution. He estimates half a million Christians by the end of the first century and 4 to 5 million by the end of the third. By the time it became the religion of the empire the Church numbered somewhere in the region of 10 million out of the 50 million in the whole of the empire – no longer little house churches led by charismatic prophetic characters! New ministries begin to emerge to deal with the new reality. The catechumenate emerges to develop and safeguard the identity and spirit of the community, and an emerging sacramental practice of reconciliation copes with those not able to live up to its moral life.

The bishop emerges as the primary minister in the local church, drawing to himself some of the influence previously exercised by apostles and prophets working to preserve the *unity* of the body of Christ. He is counselled by a group of presbyters, from among whose number he may have been elected. Deacons handle the day-to-day practical matters of feeding the poor. The reality of martyrdom acted as an egalitarian principle and it was the martyr confessor who had the highest status in the Church, not bishop or presbyter.

FROM STATE CHURCH TO COLLAPSE OF THE EMPIRE
(AD 313–500)

Christianity became tolerated in 311 via an edict of the emperor Galerius, followed in 313 by the emperor Constantine's Edict of Milan. By 381 Theodosius was able to declare Christianity the state religion of all the peoples of the Roman empire. This is the period when the presbyterate becomes sacralized and the term 'sacerdos', with all its overtones of the sacral (and the set-apart) is used as normative for the priest. Effectively ministry is reduced to that of bishop, priests and still powerful deacons, with emerging monasticism linked more to these than to the laity. At the beginning of the period priests and bishops had to be elected with the assent of the lay people. Yet by the Council of Chalcedon (451) bishops were being chosen by fellow bishops following a certain amount of consultation.

By the fifth century the term 'laity' had come to refer to Christians who were not clerics. Priests were seen as consecrated to the sacred ministry, with celibacy valued by those who aspired to be truly spiritual. The justification for this derived from the Old Testament Levitical ritual service of the temple combined with more dualist neoplatonic philosophy which downplayed the material and physical. Ministry is no longer seen as a 'normal' part of lay life. And although the Church's history since is blessed with all sorts of inspired movements of new ministry (such as those founded by Francis of Assisi, Mary Ward, Angela Merici and Jean-Marie de Chantel), it is remarkable how quickly, for different reasons, they become removed from the secular world which they originally served.

Vatican II and Beyond

MINISTRY AND MINISTRIES

Ministry is the gift of the Spirit; it is ecclesial, and is ordered to mission in the world, and yet ministries, at least in Britain, have tended to be linked to liturgical functions. However, *all* the baptized are mandated to participate in ministry. This calls for a recognition of the richness of the gifts of the Spirit and a renewed discernment of the presence of the Holy Spirit. Interesting models are available: in the United Kingdom, Salford's Sacramental Programme; Carlo

Maria Martini's attempt to open up the shared prayerful reading of Scripture in the diocese of Milan; the work of Helder Camara, Arns and Lorschneider in South America in terms of the development of base communities and their liberationist reading of the Scriptures. The emphasis here, then, is on priest and bishop enabling, recognizing and calling into being various ministries within the one eucharistic fellowship of a communion of churches which is essential if the Church is to be faithful to its apostolic origins and mission.

Vatican II provided a reassessment of the nature and function of the ordained ministry and of the episcopate in particular. The most distinct changes in this reflection were:

- The return to a patristic emphasis on episcopacy as fullness of priesthood and not merely the addition of office or privilege.
- The role of priests and bishops as only understandable in relation to one another.
- A conviction that the ordained ministry has an apostolic and Christological dimension.

Within Vatican II the threefold ministry of Jesus as teacher/ prophet, priest/sanctifier, and pastor/king is seen as the foundation of all Christian ministry.

> It was for this purpose that God sent his Son, whom he appointed heir of all things (Hebrews 1.2), that he might be teacher, king, and priest of all, the head of the new and universal people of God's sons.
>
> *(Lumen Gentium* n. 13)

The Council interprets the threefold ministry as the will of the Father in the incarnation of the Son, and sees this threefold mission as characteristic of the life of all the baptized. As the Church is the reflection of Christ in the world, so the ministry of Jesus is to be reflected in its ministry. The emphasis is, therefore, Christ-centred rather than Church-centred.

While reserving the word *ministerium* to bishops, priests and deacons, Vatican II used a variety of terms for the ministries of the laity – *munus, missio, charisma, apostolatus* (the most common) and *officium* – thus maintaining a distinction between the ordained ministry while recognizing anew the call of all the baptized to the work of mission and service. This distinction, however, has never been clearly defined.

When Pope Paul VI restructured the ministries of acolyte and reader, he suggested that some countries include them alongside other ministries within the local church. Thus a semi-formal expansion of ministries took place in some developing countries, where there may be pastoral assistants but no pastors.

Some dioceses have lay facilitators or coordinators of ministry. We have become familiar with parish sisters, and female canon lawyers. Increasingly teams of trained laity undertake the delicate questioning required by marriage tribunals. Thus our perspective and expectation of ministry is changing. New ministries have emerged in the fields of education, youth service, care for the terminally ill (the hospice movement), and there are all sorts of new ministries relating to liturgy (music ministry, welcome ministry, etc.).

Despite the encouragement of radical social encyclicals, the Christian social apostolate (the Cardijn Movements, YCW, YCS, MCW, etc.) has suffered a steady decline. It has lacked sustained official support, without which little seems able to thrive in England, and its demise is perhaps one of the sharpest indicators of just how assimilated the Catholic community has become to the individualism of contemporary English culture.

THE REDISCOVERY OF THE LOCAL CHURCH

To counter the exaggerated view of the Pope as the bishop of the world, the Second Vatican Council defined the Church as primarily a local entity gathered around its bishop (*Lumen Gentium* nn. 27, 26, 23). Thus the universal Church was presented as the worldwide network of local churches, rich in variety of practice, yet in reciprocal communion with one another, rather than uniformly ordered to some higher authoritative centre. There is no higher form of ministry in the Church than that of the local bishop.

Vatican II gave the charter to the local church, seeing it as precisely the real Church of Christ in a particular place. So in a contextual reading of Scripture, the bishop receives insight into the gospel he witnesses to from his community and draws the local community into a '*conspiratio fidelium et pastorum*' (Newman, *On Consulting the Faithful*, pp. 65f.; and *Dei Verbum* 10). The emphasis here then returns to the bishop's teaching authority as a *testificatio fidei* rather than a *determinatio fidei* which tends to situate pope and bishops independently of their communities (Gaillardetz, 1992).

The emphasis on local churches in reciprocal relationship has specific implications for episcopal ministry. The Council raised the patristic model of episcopacy above the juridical model of recent centuries which had in many ways treated the bishop as chief priest. The renewed theology of episcopacy makes it clear that the bishop's call mediated by the Church comes from God in the Spirit rather than from the bishop of Rome. The theological shift has thus been to a renewed sense of the college of bishops with the Pope as the centre of unity with each bishop responsible both for the unity of the local church and carrying a shared responsibility for the unity of the world Church. While this renewed model of the college of bishops is a manifestation of the spirit of *koinonia* it nevertheless contains unresolved tensions.

There is an uneasy mix of the theology of the sacramental model of the first millennium with the juridical model of the second. The Roman Congregation for the Doctrine of the Faith is, I think, more aware of the danger of overemphasizing the first (federalist) rather than the second (juridical), with its temptation to centralist tendencies. However, the theology is clear: the local church is not a derivative of the worldwide Church.

EPISCOPAL AND PRESBYTERAL COLLEGIALITY

In the dogmatic Constitution on the Church, *Lumen Gentium*, it is clearly stated that bishops receive their power from Christ rather than from the Pope. 'The Bishops lead the partner Churches entrusted to them as substitutes and ambassadors for Christ ... they are not to be understood as substitutes for the Bishop of Rome' (n. 27). It is precisely the bishop who is seen as successor to the apostles, as a member of the apostolic college.

Notice the renewed emphasis on the relationship between the bishops who are seen as having a collegial responsibility for the whole Church, with the Pope exercising a particular ministry of serving the right ordering of unity *within* the college *rather than over it* (*Lumen Gentium* n. 22). At the time of the Council a fear that papal authority might be undermined led to the various cautionary amendments added to the text late in the day in order to protect papal primacy. Nevertheless, the Council bears witness to a move from a predominantly juridical understanding (the power of order) to a more sacramental understanding, based on a vision of the Church from the base rather than the apex. The importance of collegiality lies in the renewal of the communal relational model of apostolic service focused in the local church but with worldwide implications in terms of communion.

Just as a conciliar theology sees the bishop as the recipient of a charism received directly from God yet exercised within the relationship of collegial communion, so it sees priests as empowered by Christ rather than the bishop (*Presbyterorum Ordinis* nn. 12, 2, 5; *Ad*

Gentes n. 39). The priest acts in the name of Christ serving the diocese with his bishop. This collegial quality of the presbyterium around its bishop is referred to in terms of the priest as co-worker or collaborator with the bishop. Thus the renewal of the patristic understanding of presbyters as counsellors of the episcopos from the perspective of a shared ministry of teaching, sanctifying and leading is made.

When we examine the decrees of the Council on the laity we see a similar development. Prior to Vatican II the official model of lay apostolate (Catholic Action) was the laity as the outreach of the hierarchy into those areas which hierarchy cannot reach: civil society, politics, economics, the family, etc. It was a model of dependence and subordination with power centred in a monarchical manner on bishops and pope. While this model bore rich fruit in some places it was disastrous in others, encouraging a naive docility to instruction, even when that instruction demonstrated a regrettably limited awareness of social reality.

Vatican II broke the bonds of such infantile dependency. All the baptized are called to an apostolate by Christ himself through baptism, confirmation and eucharist. The lay apostolate thus constitutes the normal participation of baptized Christians in the saving mission of the Church.

THE CHURCH AS ICON OF TRINITARIAN LIFE

Like the Trinity the Church's reality lies in an essential orientation towards relationship. Our God is a being-in-communion. If we share *koinonia* with God in Christ then we will find ourselves in *koinonia* with each other. Christian unity and fruitful collaboration will come through relational holiness rather than the implementation of new structures. The Church is constituted by relationship to and for one another; to and for creation. The German phrase is 'Ein Christ ist kein Christ' – 'a solitary Christian is no Christian'. Faith is a reciprocal, communal reality.

However, those of us imbued with a pre-conciliar spirituality were taught to think in terms of the spiritual life as very much 'me and God', with the emphasis on saving my soul. For this reason the Council emphasized dialogue as part of what it is to be church: difference within unity, as in the Trinity.

The patristic writings refer to the reality of the Church in its essential mystery as *koinonia/communio*. The term is used by St Paul to describe our relationship to God through Christ and through the Spirit within the Eucharist. In order to acquire a richer understanding of *communio*, then, we need to reflect upon our relationship with God. The Church is called to be *communio* because that is what God is.

Since the Extraordinary Synod of 1985, *communio* has moved centre stage and has become an umbrella concept beneath which Catholics, Orthodox and Anglicans have increasingly found themselves, although the usage shifts and varies.

Lumen Gentium sees *communio*, above all, as a participation in the divine life made real for us in Jesus Christ. We share in his unique communion through the Holy Spirit who dwells in our hearts and within the body of believers and who draws the churches into a further communion. The focus of *communio* then is the nature of God and our communion with and in God. The focus of faith then is not primarily the Church but is God and life in God. If we are led into *koinonia* with God in Christ we will necessarily be in *koinonia* with each other, so the initial vertical reference becomes fleshed out in the horizontal everyday reality of Christian sacramental life.

The Church is, thus, sent out into the world to reveal the mystery of communion. The unity of the Trinity revealed in the scandalous particularity of the incarnation, in the working man Jesus of Nazareth, and the wonderful work of the Spirit who draws seemingly disparate voices into relationship as at the first Pentecost.

EUCHARISTIC FOCUS

It is above all in the Eucharist that the Church touches and is touched by the Trinitarian *communio/koinonia*. In the proclaimed scriptures we hear of Word made flesh in Israel's history and in the life of one man. In Jesus' prayer to the Father we are drawn into his sacrifice, entering the dark mystery of the cross, and uniting ourselves in thanksgiving in the Spirit as we are opened up to receive the new life of the risen Lord, the pilgrim's fare, strengthening us to open our minds, hearts and lives to those around us. In Augustine's words: 'A sign of unity and a bond of love' (*Tractatus in Johannis Evangelium* Ch. 6.13, CpChL 36, 266). To receive the eucharistic body of Christ is to have fellowship with the body of Christ, the Church. Augustine sums it up:

> So if you yourselves be the body of Christ and his members, then on the eucharistic table lies your own mystery ... You shall be what you see, and you shall receive what you are.
>
> (*Sermo* CCLXXII, PL 38.1247)

Here in the Eucharist and in what flows into and from it, the real God, and our own mystery in God, is revealed anew. The challenge is for structures, institution and rite to manifest this ever more clearly.

In relationship to the Eucharist the bishop has a particular ministry – that of servant. He is identified in a particular way with *the* servant, the Father's Son, and drawn in a particular way into his passion, which is the inevitable consequence of accepting the call to be servant. This call takes the bishop where he might not prefer to go: into the darkness of child abuse, of priestly abusers and falling vocations. He is called to be the servant of the Lord who is both above the community and within it. This presidency of service at the heart of communion is a focus for the whole communion even of those who self-evidently distance themselves from the bishop: left or right, rationalist or fideist, liberal or traditional, a communion beyond the merely juridical, social or formally doctrinal, a communion at the level of mystery.

It seems to me then that the best episcopal service of *communio* would be the fostering of a true celebration of eucharist throughout the local church. A focusing on the preaching of the word, challenging a prophetic community toward a mature and responsible witness in the world. A service of *communio* that coordinates and guides and inspires, rescuing God's people from the passivity to which they have grown accustomed and rescuing God's servants from the danger of an empty hyperactivity. The Trinity will not become the luminous centre of Christian life until the Church reflects the mystery of the divine life, unity rather than uniformity, distinctions rather than separation.

THE MAGISTERIUM OF THE WHOLE PEOPLE OF GOD

What is the relationship between ordained ministers and the baptized as regards the teaching office of Jesus? If all share in this office through baptism, can the magisterium be limited to pope and bishops?

Communio was a basic ecclesiological concept in the early Church. Through baptism the believer was initiated into the communion of the triune life of God and simultaneously into the communion of believers. For the first thousand years of the Church's life the bishop was ordained to a local community. Unattached bishops were anathema. The bishop served the ecclesial communion receiving insight into the gospel and tradition, to which he bears witness, from the life of the local community. This demands a contextual reading of the word of God in which the text of people's own lives, and the context in which they live, provokes the gospel to render unsuspected levels of meaning. Talk with a mature woman about the debilitating effect of long-term problems with the menstrual cycle and Mark 5.25–34 will never be the same again. I opened up this Gospel recently at a day of recollection for thirty ladies from a local Guild of Our Lady. The youngest woman present was in her fifties, and one was nearly 90. They were spinsters, wives, widows, mothers, grandmothers. The ensuing discussion, which they had not anticipated, was extraordinarily rich in a Christian wisdom from a woman's perspective: wisdom seldom available to the Church but which can become available when the bishop unites the local community in what Newman called a '*conspiratio fidelium et pastorum*', an idea echoed in *Dei Verbum* n. 10. There is a dialectic here between the episcopal witness and its fleshed-out verification within the life of the community itself. It is precisely in communion with the Spirit-indwelt local community that the bishop is nourished in the apostolic tradition. His teaching authority is not delegated by the flock but is grounded in his relation to it.

Communion at the level of the episcopal college requires the communion of local bishop and presbyterium. A communion ecclesiology places greater emphasis on the bishop reflecting back and communicating what he has received.

BISHOPS AND POPE – TWO SUPREME AUTHORITIES

Vatican I's *Pastor Aeternus* described the Pope as the supreme authority in the Church. Vatican II affirmed this but also stated that the college of bishops also possessed supreme authority.

> This power of the supreme pontiff by no means detracts from that ordinary and immediate power of episcopal jurisdiction, by which bishops, who have succeeded to the place of the apostles by appointment of the holy Spirit, tend and govern individually the particular flocks which have been assigned to them. On the contrary, this power of theirs is asserted, supported and defended by the supreme and universal pastor; for St Gregory the Great says: 'My honour is the honour of the whole church. My honour is the steadfast strength of my brethren. Then do I receive true honour, when it is denied to none of those to whom honour is due.'
>
> (Tanner, vol. II, p. 814)

While Vatican I did not intend to undermine the bishops it certainly failed to provide a rich and inclusive theology of episcopal ministry. It left us with two supreme authorities, the yet-to-be-worked-out implications of the Pope as head of the college, and the question of a possible solo act of supreme authority by the Pope.

PLANETARY CONSCIOUSNESS

Vatican II enabled us to face the real world as the place where the Spirit of God is at work in the midst of economics and politics, of power struggles and vested interests. It offered a more realistic and in some ways a humbler vision. Such a vision is underwritten in *Gaudium et Spes*, *Lumen Gentium*, *Ad Gentes* and *Nostra Aetate*. It was anticipated by that great encyclical of John XXIII *Pacem in Terris* and again by the vision of the early John Paul II in *Redemptor Hominis*. A vision of men and women walking purposefully alongside their brothers and sisters in history. Brothers and sisters from other churches, religions, worldviews, sharing their burdens, their hopes and sorrows.

The Catholicism in which I grew up was more interested in the next world than in this one and I, as a child, was more interested in saving my own soul rather than saving the planet! Such a viewpoint, however, could not really survive *Gaudium et Spes*. Time has moved on and scholars and theologians such as Hans Küng, David Tracey, Leonardo Boff and Jürgen Moltmann are appealing for the development of a new planetary ethic, a paradigm shift to a new planetary consciousness.

DIFFERENT MODELS OF CHURCH AND HIERARCHY

Since the Council there has been a growing tension between centralized authority focused in the Vatican Curial offices which prefer to deal with individual bishops and dioceses and the growing collaboration between the college of bishops in national, international and continental conferences which express Vatican II's renewed emphasis on collegiality. The Curial model is still based on a predominantly vertical vision of hierarchy with bishop responsible to pope, as vicar of Christ; priest to bishop and people to priest. Jurisdiction and the call to ministry are seen as being exercised from above. The theology underpinning such a model was deliberately abandoned by Vatican II as belonging to a different era in which the Church saw itself as a community set apart, a ghetto community embattled and under attack.

The gradually emerging collegial structures are based on a renewed theology of communion/*koinonia* – in which the foundational reality of life in Christ through baptism is the source and focus of ministry. All the initiated are called to lives that are priestly, prophetic and royal with that dignity that is the quality of all the beloved sons and daughters of the Father God. The underpinning theology is richly Trinitarian and clearly influenced by the Eastern fathers. It is fully capable of expressing unity in diversity and of seeing pluralism as necessary to express the sheer richness of revelation in Christ. This implies a collaborative practice in which ministry is seen in terms of the relationship of bishop and priest to the varieties of service of the whole community. This is, however, a very different model from that with which most Catholics are familiar.

In the emerging collegial model the primary focus of priesthood and ministry is that of the Letter to the Hebrews, where Christ is portrayed as the one true priest with the resulting priesthood of all believers (Hebrews 9.15). The focus is on the essential humanity of Jesus which we share with him (Hebrews 4.15—5.8). Ministry derives from the Spirit-indwelt community and exists for its sake. There is no reference to a superior ministry.

Cyprian spoke of this in AD 250 in terms of the Spirit of God being seen to be at work *throughout* the community rather than 'from the top down'. Cardinal John Henry Newman's reflections of the *sensus fidei* indicates something of the experience of the early community in Jerusalem whose leaders had to be challenged by Paul the outsider. Priestly ordination specifies a ministry of service within the community, a call to a particular relationship, a particular type of service (Mark 3.13–19). And it is a ministry that, according to *Presbyterorum Ordinis* 4, is word-based and prophetic.

This ecclesiology of accompaniment has prophets like Charles de Foucauld, who lived alongside the Bedouin in the North African desert, treating them as brothers. It is an ecclesiology involving all the people of God in open listening and learning – bishop, priests, laymen and women. It has been celebrated sacramentally in the 'World Day of Prayer' at Assisi in 1986, when Pope John Paul II invited the religious leaders of the world to pray alongside one another.

Many different groups are calling today for an ecclesiology of orthopraxis rather than simply orthodoxy. 'Walking the walk', instead of only 'talking the talk'. The First Letter of Peter offers a model that anticipates in expression the joyful and enthusiastic vision of *Lumen Gentium* and *Gaudium et Spes*. Yet it was written in a time of trial and suffering (Rome in AD 80–90). It offers a vision of participation within the world, rather than flight from it. It suggests that men and women can be fascinated and changed through the example of Christian life lived in the midst of everyday reality. It is a wonderful restatement of the central thrust of Jesus' own life and ministry and his insistence on God as *Abba* – the God of the everyday.

Such an ecclesiology in our world will therefore necessarily be focused on the little ones, the marginal – it is they who provoke us to be church. Their sacrament is Lourdes, where the sick, the broken and the powerless are at the centre and give meaning and purpose to the rest of us. The greatest obstacle to faith in our world is not lack of orthodoxy but rather lack of such true service: orthopraxis. Gregory of Nyssa put it well: 'Concepts create idols, only wonder grasps anything' (PG 44.377). If we enter the Eucharist in wonder then our minds and hearts will expand to discover our own mystery and that of all God's children.

It seems to me then that the best service of *communio* would be the fostering of a true celebration of eucharist throughout the local church, focusing on the preaching of the whole word of the Eucharist, that reaches its clearest focus in the presence of Christ through the power of the Spirit. A prophetic word challenging a prophetic community toward a mature and responsible witness in the world, rather than encouraging a return to a holy huddle.

The Trinity will not be the luminous centre of Christian life till the life of the Church reflects the mystery of the divine life, at the heart of which is a unity without uniformity, distinction without separation.

Conclusion

A rich theology of the episcopate is emerging in our time. It is situated within the threefold ministry which characterizes all the baptized. It is understood as the fullness of priesthood within the midst of the Church in necessary mutual relationship to the other ordained ministries, as a ministry at the service of the mission of all the faithful, enabling, inspiring and leading, always from within rather than from above, as a ministry which sees the pastoral charge of the local church as integral to full membership of the college of bishops. The Pope, within the college, is the one through whom the community is called to know its own deepest reality. The bishop's whole life is at the service of community: attending to it; encouraging and inspiring; listening and drawing forth its strengths and weaknesses; sharing what he sees and knows locally through the presbyterium, and internationally through the episcopal college.

This rich vision is based upon the Lord's own mission, the manner in which he worked with his close collaborators; the communion he built in table fellowship and inclusive teaching. There are many obstacles in the way of developing such a model of episcopacy, but such a model is better adapted to the needs of the body of Christ in the service of the world.

Congar suggests it takes fifty years for a council to deliver its fruits; if that is so then this generation of bishops have a key role in enabling that to happen. Present problems are the basis of future rich opportunities. The Holy Spirit was poured out upon the whole apostolic group; the call today is for the whole episcopate to work together, that the Spirit so richly visible in our time may not be frustrated.

References

Bernier, P. (1992) *Ministry in the Church: A Historical and Pastoral Approach*, Connecticut: Twenty-Third Publications.

Corpus Christianorum, Series Latina (1953ff.), Brepols:Turnholt.

Denzinger, H. and Schönmetzer, A. (1976) *Enchiridion Symbolorum*, 36th edn, Frieburg im Breisgau.

Gaillardetz, R. (1992) *Witnesses to Faith: Community, Infallibility and the Ordinary Magisterium of Bishops*, New York: Paulist Press.

Käsemann, E. (1968) 'Ministry and Community in the New Testament', in *Essays on New Testament Themes*, London: SCM.

Tanner, N. (1990) *Decrees of the Ecumenical Councils*, London: Sheed & Ward.

Chapter Ten

CONTEMPORARY EUROPEAN VALUES AND 'AUTHORITY IN THE CATHOLIC CHURCH'

David Barker

Born in Kent, David Barker is an economics graduate. Following brief experience in commerce, the civil service and education, he worked for a number of years in the industrial policy division of the National Economic Development Office. From 1972 to 1998 he acted as adviser to a number of British and European charitable foundations and ran the Derwent Consultancy in London, which specializes in advisory services to churches and charities. He has published on industrial and social policy, charity law and administration and the sociology of religion. He has also contributed to the reports published by the European Values Group examining the moral and social conditions of the European population.

Introduction

Prepared by a lapsed social scientist, but still practising Catholic, with an interest in values research, this chapter draws upon the European Values Surveys, the work of the Queens Foundation Working Party, the opinions of informed commentators and the testimony of active Catholics. It represents a view of the evidence from somebody who is not a theologian or pastor. Inevitably, it focuses more on identifying the problems of authority and governance than on celebrating solutions. It endeavours to address the issues directly and honestly without ducking them. Consequently, it is 'hard-hitting' in places but it is not intended to be hostile or confrontational. The range of topics covered is broad because, whatever the 'point of entry' chosen to begin to explore questions of authority in the Church, one is inevitably drawn both to Rome and to home, as also to both theory and practice. The issues are complex; opinions are diverse and consensus on the best way forward is difficult to achieve. The author's preferences are apparent but the aim of the paper is to provide a basis for constructive discussion.

Social Context: Cultural Shift and its Implications

CULTURE SHIFT

In his assessment of 'culture shift' in advanced industrial society, Inglehart suggests that:

> what people want out of life is changing. These changes are re-shaping people's feelings of national identity, their sexual and re-ligious norms and what they want in a job. The changes are occurring so gradually that they generally escape notice, but their longer term consequences are massive.
>
> (Inglehart, 1990)

He indicates that population replacement is an important element in this process and points out that by the year 2000 half the popula-tion of Europe will have been replaced by younger generations with different (what he calls post-materialist) values, which mark a change from concerns with security to an emphasis on self-expres-sion. The European Values Surveys in 1981 and 1990 pointed to some of the implications of these changes including a growing em-phasis (particularly among those aged under 50) on the following:

> personal autonomy and self-expression, personal growth, openness in public institutions, participation in those decisions that affect people's lives, self-reliance, protest and an emphasis on human rights, toleration of 'deviant' private morality but intolerance of public behaviour which encroaches on the quality of common life.
>
> (Barker, 1993)

These changes are apparent within Britain as among its European neighbours and North American cousins, though – with the possible exception of the increase in the proportion of the 'unchurched' in the population – not marked by dramatic changes as, for example, in attitudes to sexuality in Spain.

The evidence confirms the importance of generational replace-ment in value change. It also points to the influence of gender. For example, women exhibited stricter moral standards than men in 1981. By 1990 female attitudes approximated to those of males, whose standards, by that time, had become more relaxed. Again, while women are more orthodox in matters of religious belief than men, the differences are narrowing. The high value placed on family life is accompanied by a growing unwillingness to tolerate unsatisfactory marital relationships and a desire to see marriage and family life as vehicles for self-expression and personal development.

In terms of social relations Europeans trust the members of their immediate families but are cautious about outsiders. Attitudes to neighbours are complex with significant national variations. The British are close to the European norm. In general, it is anti-social behaviour rather than racial or religious identity which leads to intolerance, and attitudes are hardening towards unacceptable behaviour. Significantly, public expectations of politicians are rising, but trust in politicians and governments has fallen in Britain since the 1970s (Barker, 1993; Curtice and Jowell, 1997).

Drawing upon the annual British Social Attitudes Surveys, Ahrendt and Young (1994) concluded that, whereas in 1989 about half the population endorsed certain authoritarian attitudes, the proportion had fallen to two-fifths by 1993. A substantial majority of the population remained tough on crime and were concerned to teach children respect for 'traditional British values' and obedience to authority. Yet, attitudes to unemployment and welfare issues had become more compassionate and people were less condemnatory towards homosexuals and people with AIDS. Authoritarianism is associated with increasing age, low educational attainment, Conservative party affiliation and membership of social classes III–V. Religion also plays a part, but the correlation is weaker than for the other factors.

Throughout Europe and North America, confidence in both democratic and autocratic institutions eroded in the 1980s. The sole exception was major companies, which grew in popularity, though public criticism has since increased. Dissatisfaction with the political process and diminished institutional confidence coupled with a desire for self-expression is consistent with the apparent greater willingness of people of all ages to affirm or engage in spontaneous, predominantly lawful, acts of protest (Barker, 1993; Curtice and Jowell, 1997).

IMPLICATIONS FOR THE CHURCHES

Greater endorsement of autonomy, participation and protest among women and men, together with a demand for openness in public institutions, signal a fundamental change in the relations of lay people with the Church. From a recent survey of the Catholic laity in four European countries (including Poland and Italy), the

USA and the Philippines, Fr Greeley and Michael Hout concluded that:

> The Catholic laity hopes for a new pope who will be attentive to the realities of their lives and open to change. He should achieve these goals by giving autonomy to the local bishops, appointing lay advisers, returning to the practice of electing local bishops, ordaining women and allowing priests to marry. If enacted, these reforms will make the church a more pluralistic and democratic institution.
>
> (Greeley and Hout, 1997)

Subsequent results for Germany suggests that 'German Catholics are the most favourable of all to change' ('Notebook', *The Tablet*, 1997).

These emerging values and attitudes are consistent with studies which point to the relationship between psychological well-being and a sense of freedom and control over one's life (e.g. Myers, 1992). They sit uneasily, however, with the prevailing institutional culture of the Catholic Church. As Markham recently suggested:

> As we face the next millennium, we find a profound analysis of our contemporary situation set out in the encyclicals written by Pope John Paul II. However, I have argued that these encyclicals are marred by their failure to acknowledge any 'shades of grey'. The ethical methodology is traditional: the positions taken are firm and uncompromising; and the recognition of complexity is rarely conceded.
>
> (Markham, 1997)

He notes Professor Ronald Preston's comment that 'No other empirical sources are mentioned. No flaws in church teaching are admitted.'

The Values Survey confirmed that the institutional Church continues to play an important role in European life, but its significance is diminishing as a gradual process of disengagement leads to a growing proportion of first- or second-generation unchurched adults, a decline in religiosity and erosion of religious belief, especially among the young. Europeans accept a limited public role for the churches but reject interference in their intimate personal lives and in government policy. Confidence in the institutional Church remains high among the elderly, relative to other public institutions (in 1990 it ranked third out of 13 institutions among those over 50 years of age), and those on the political right, but not among the young (for whom it was the least popular institution for those aged under 35 years). By 1990 only one in seven parents aged under 35 years believed it important to develop religious faith in children. They were also more likely than older parents to emphasize qualities such as independence, imagination and self-control. The growth in the unchurched is particularly marked in Britain (up from 9 per cent in 1981 to 42 per cent in 1990), Belgium (32 per cent), France (39 per cent) and the Netherlands (49 per cent). Reviewing these findings in 1992 (prior to the present more youthful Labour administration), I suggested that:

> The morally autonomous Europeans, disengaged from the churches, disenchanted with democratic institutions and the political process, demanding greater involvement in the decisions which affect their lives and willing to take direct political action to achieve their aims, pose a fundamental challenge to political and religious leaders. Confidence in church and parliament is eroding. The responses offered to contemporary moral, social and environmental problems are seen as inadequate. Leaders are an elderly and remote group whose messages do not resonate with the young. They are in danger of addressing only their shadows. Fundamental reform of political and religious structures and a revised notion of the obligations of citizenship may be necessary to reintegrate political, religious and community life in a way consistent with more egalitarian social relations.
>
> (Barker, 1992)

Indeed (at the risk of distorting the complexity and richness of the European reality), it seemed to me as a broad generalization that those aged under 35 years (who would be middle-aged in 2000) inhabited a different moral and cultural universe to the over 50s. The two universes were not necessarily opposed to each other. They exhibited different priorities, were not in communication and functioned independently.

In the case of the Catholic Church, the values and attitudes of the 'younger' universe have been perceived as a threat to the institution, and 'difference' is frequently interpreted as opposition. The emerging values and attitudes are rejected as undermining faith and morals.

In his study of the Vatican drawing upon interviews with over 100 officials, Fr Reese (1996) comments 'the possibility of contemporary developments is frightening to an institution that prizes stability, tradition, and magisterial authority'. In appointing bishops, 'orthodoxy and church discipline are crucial. A priest supporting the ordination of women, optional priestly celibacy, or birth control will not be made a bishop.' Church leaders are members of the older (and, as Inglehart claims, disappearing) universe. Canon McNamara's vision (1996) of the raised papal voice becoming ever fainter as the barque of Peter drifts away from the people over the horizon may not be so far from the truth. In time, present attitudes may well be 'grown out of' the institutional Church; but what will replace them and will other elements be lost that may take generations to recapture? In the meantime, Fr Reese suggests:

> Many in the Vatican, including John Paul, believe that more authoritative statements will accentuate Catholic identity and make the church more attractive in the religious confusion. Some Vatican officials believe that the church would be better off without dissident Catholics, who simply sow confusion. A smaller, more faithful church, even a remnant, is the future they see for the church.
>
> (Reese, 1996)

The Pope may have a point. Many young people (yet to have their enthusiasm dulled by institutional constraints) continue to be inspired by his direct appeal to them. Morris, author of a recent study of the American church, comments:

> If you listen to what liberal theologians say, it sounds very much like what Episcopalians were saying thirty years ago, and there aren't any Episcopalians left. Churches that adopt the culture die. Anybody who wants to reform Catholicism should read what Roger Stark has to say, namely, that only high-tension religions survive in this country.
>
> (Morris, 1997)

Others question whether hard doctrine and tough practice are essential to Catholic identity and ask if people seek, rather, hard doctrine coupled with reasonable church practice (of authority and in governance), which meets the needs and social temper of the times and place. Rome is perhaps unwilling to make the distinction, insisting that certain practices be regarded as dogma, and sanctioning those who disagree.

Given the social context, however, the Vatican strategy outlined by Fr Reese is probably doomed to failure in the West. As the Irish President Mary McAleese points out:

> Consent to the processes of authority, rather than to the authority itself, is intensely problematic. The roar from behind the barricades in Rome is a bluff, and it is being called. Importantly, it is not being called out of spite, nor out of gratuitous mischief-

making. It is being called out of an impulse which is Christ-centred and which is determined to shift the gravitational pull of the Church back to an authentic vision of Christ, and away from narrow clerical institutionalism.

(McAleese, 1995)

Fr Cosgrave (1995) suggests that what is required in the Western church is not formal democracy so much as an ethos of democracy; requiring norms of consultation, collaboration, accountability and due process – an argument adopted also by Connor and Lindsell in the present volume.

Assumptions in the Institutional Response

AN INAPPROPRIATE PSYCHOLOGICAL MODEL

The response of the institution appears to be driven more by fear than by love. As Dominian points out in the present volume, the exercise of authority in the contemporary Church is frequently inappropriate to the needs of mature Christian adults. The dominant institutional approach, he suggests, is based on a psychological model of infantile obedience and dependency – an extension of parent–child relationships using fear and guilt as sanctions. Yet Christ's relationship with his Father and obedience to his authority was based on love, arising out of the certainty of that love and equality of worth expressed in freedom and service; a willingness to make himself available to others.

From his study of parish life in the Birmingham Archdiocese, Ryan (1996) confirms that immaturity in religious life seems to have been an intrinsic part of Catholic identity. Priests seeking to delegate power and build up a community of faith who now criticize parishioners for their unwillingness to accept responsibility are, in fact, reaping a harvest the seeds of which were sown by them and their predecessors many years ago.

They had the power: over resources, over consciences, over education, over the common life of the community. They used that power to achieve what they thought the Catholic priesthood was there to achieve: identikit Catholics, pressed from a mould: pious, moral, docile, obedient – and passive. The ideal Catholic was the child.

(Ryan, 1996)

Believing, but non-practising, adults, he suggests, having been treated as children, may identify religion as something for children and may restrict their religious involvement to their children's education.

DOMINATING POWER

Mahoney (1985) indicates that values such as faithfulness, mutual respect, understanding and tolerance which emerge from the Values Survey as essential elements in a successful marriage 'all appear also to be particular expressions of that *koinonia* ethics to which the church is called, and of which man, made in God's image, may be thought to possess intimations'. In contrast to earlier conceptions, a modern and more dynamic understanding of the divine image in humankind emphasizes the calling

> to reflect in his own being the interpersonal life which is at the centre of Divine Being as Father, Son and Holy Spirit. Man's calling from creation is to live in relationship, whether with God, or in the 'covenant' of marriage and family, or in the 'communion' of the Church, or in the wider nexus of the whole human family.
>
> (Mahoney, 1985)

Fr McLoughlin in the present collection suggests that a relational, trinitarian, model of authority (patristic, pre-schism, pre-Reformation) is authentic and necessary, emphasizing faith as a reciprocal reality and the bishop immersed in, nourished by and reflecting back to his community what he has received 'from the witness of the lived faith of the Church'. Bishop Matthew Clark (1997) elaborates this, emphasizing that the bishop must listen attentively for the word of God not only among the strong and noble but also among the poor, weak, marginalized and alienated in the Church 'in order to testify before the Great Church to the faith and practice of his own particular church'.

Gaillardetz sets authority within the context of this ecclesiology of communion as follows:

> The exercise of power and authority in the church can only be understood relationally . . . an ecclesiology of communion grounded in the triune God admits the existence of a stable differentiation of ecclesial relations and ministries; it does reject any differentiation or ordering that subordinates one relation or ministry to another . . . all relationships are mutual and reciprocal.
>
> (Gaillardetz, 1997)

Fr McLoughlin refers to the procedures of the May 1997 Vocations Conference in Rome as an example of 'how dominating power can be maintained through legitimate church structures, the existence of which is justified because they serve the Church's unity' (1997). To these concerns one might also add the use of language, both technical and theological, as a means of dominating power. Without the language you are devoid of influence. The periodic abuse of power within the Church illustrates the human and structural limitations of a theologically concise, biblically based but, nevertheless, ideal vision of church that any *communio* model represents.

SUBORDINATION OF WOMEN

An emphasis on relational authority characterized by mutuality, reciprocity, love and justice is consistent with the search in feminist theology for appropriate ways to speak about God in a church which many women experience as 'pervaded by sexism with its twin faces of patriarchy and androcentrism' (Johnson, 1992).

If the socio-linguist Tannen is correct (her evidence is partly anecdotal and her reference group is mainly drawn from middle-class Americans of predominantly European background), the adjustment will be problematic for a male-dominated hierarchy which has little knowledge or experience of and does not appear to value, intimate communication with women.

Tannen (1986) suggests that interpersonal communication is essentially cross-cultural and influenced as much by gender as by religion, ethnicity, class or geography. Consequently, it is ambiguous and misunderstanding inevitable without care and sensitivity. Men, she believes, have a tendency to engage in impersonal 'report' talk, women in 'rapport' talk, drawing upon personal experience. Attention to words alone is insufficient. Meaning is negotiated and interpreted through 'metamessages' which depend upon the relationship between the parties, their attitudes, status, methods of communication, conversational devices and body language employed. Women pay more attention to metamessages than men. Significant gender differences are apparent from childhood and endure into adult life. Women seek involvement, affirmation and intimacy whereas men are more likely to value independence and social distance. Drawing upon workplace experience, Tannen notes that the language of authority and the metaphors used are masculine. Men are more likely to assert their authority than women, who typically downplay it and try to build a consensus – to their disadvantage. Women are comfortable giving and receiving advice – whereas men prefer to give it (even, she suggests, when they don't know what they are talking about).

They like the centre-stage position of 'expert' rather than attentive listener, tend to talk down to women and confuse them.

Women, Sr Johnson (1992) suggests, 'seek to articulate an extensively relational self grounded in a community of free reciprocity'. The nature of God is 'inherently communio' and 'At the very deepest core of reality is a mystery of personal connectedness that constitutes the very livingness of God.' Sadly, in the Christian community, for most of its history

> women have been subordinated in theological theory and ecclesial practice at every turn ... Even as I write, women in the Catholic community are excluded from full participation in the sacramental system, from ecclesial centers of significant decision making, law making, and symbol making, and from official public leadership roles whether in governance or the liturgical assembly. They are called to honor a male savior sent by a male God whose legitimate representatives can only be male, all of which places their persons precisely as female in a peripheral role. Their femaleness is judged to be not suitable as metaphor for speech about God.
>
> (Johnson, 1992)

Are these issues being addressed? Does the will to do so exist at the highest level? Bingemer (1989) believes that we are currently witnessing an awakening of women in the Church and in theology to a deliberate decision to speak, not in isolation but through solidarity with the oppressed, in community, in church.

Nevertheless, there is far to go. Active women in particular face hard choices about perseverance or withdrawal from a situation they regard as unjust. The Church is not yet experienced as a mature relational community. Fr Cooper discovered that

> Working with various pastoral teams, eighty percent of lay ministers were competent qualified professional women. Yet pastors who were insensitive to women's issues often showed a lack of respect for the dignity of the women in their pastoral team, and failed to allocate resources for their professional development. When treated in this fashion, the dignity of women as equal partners in ministry is denied, and they are kept in a subservient role in their relationship with the pastor.
>
> (Cooper, 1993)

In church government, few women hold senior posts and, despite the fact that there are ten times as many international female congregations as there are male congregations, the Vatican authorities typically consult the male congregations on matters of significance pertaining to the women before referring to the women religious directly. Within individual congregations, as Sr Alford's (1996) account of the fragmentation of the Dominican sisters (in contrast to the friars) confirms, the sisters have 'accepted a "decentred" position in the Dominican Order', finding their 'unity, centre and identity in being recognised by the central authorities of the Friars'. She also illustrates how 'often it was the local bishops and other clerical authorities that engineered the splits between the sisters', frequently without consultation with the religious superiors, and exploited their good will and resources.

Finally, the statement in 1995 by the Congregation for the Doctrine of the Faith that the doctrine excluding the ordination of women to the priesthood 'pertains to the deposit of faith'; and that it has been infallibly taught by the ordinary and universal magisterium marks, in Fr Sullivan's view, 'the first time, that an authoritative document of the Holy See has specifically declared that a particular doctrine has been infallibly taught in this way' (1996). Fr Sullivan questions how it can be known to be an established fact that the worldwide episcopate is in agreement with the teaching of Pope John Paul II on this matter. He suggests that the CDF has not invoked the three ways of establishing that the doctrine is taught by the ordinary and universal magisterium. 'Consultation of all the bishops, the universal and constant consensus of Catholic theologians, and the common adherence of all the faithful.' The debate is not closed. Given the contemporary emphasis on autonomy, rights and protest, true internal assent to such teaching is not probable. Like *Humanae Vitae* it is unlikely to be received. Indeed, Fr Reese maintains that

> The Vatican's attempt to silence the debate over women's ordination has only succeeded in angering more women. If the church loses educated women in the twenty-first century the way it lost European working-class males in the nineteenth century, it will be in serious trouble.

> (Reese, 1996)

CENTRALIZATION

Summarizing the development of papal authority over time, Duffy (1997) concludes that 'For the first time, the Church has a papacy whose power is almost equal to its claims. This is certainly dangerous for the local life of the churches and will have to be addressed in the new millennium'. He notes that many of the characteristics of

the papacy, including control of episcopal appointments, are very
recent indeed and 'originated less in any scriptural or patristic
basis than in the vagaries of history, and in the confusion of roles
which were in theory quite distinct'. He points to the massive increase in centralization which followed the 1917 Code of Canon
Law and suggests that

> what comes by historical accident may go by historical accident.
> The present powers of the popes in such matters as episcopal ap-
> pointments are open to assessment on grounds of utility, efficiency
> and theological fitness, and might be changed on any one or all of
> these counts.
>
> (Duffy, 1997)

Markus is hesitant to apportion blame, suggesting that

> The ministerial conception of authority in the Church has not, of
> course, vanished. Upheld by popes, put into daily practice by
> dedicated bishops and clergy, it has remained at the core of ec-
> clesiastical office. The trouble lies not with persons and the way
> they exercise their authority: it inheres in the system in which
> they are placed. The monopoly of ecclesiastical power that such
> a highly centralised structure bestows on the centre can encou-
> rage arbitrary, even unjust, use. Unless curbed by opposition,
> even the possibility of challenge, it is in constant danger of corrup-
> tion. The Church's answer to increasing globalisation should be a
> return, if not quite to the parish pump, at any rate to smaller and
> simpler groupings, involving more widely dispersed and messier,
> competing, overlapping spheres of authority reposing in local
> churches, with their own bishops.
>
> (Markus, 1997)

Fr Collins (1997) suggests that a focus on communion would help to
shift the emphasis from an omnipresent papacy and Rome-centred
ecclesiology to an emphasis on the local church. Important in this
context, he suggests, is the notion of the bishop of Rome exercising
a 'presidency of charity'.

> It offers a whole new model for the papacy, or, more accurately,
> the relationship of the pope to the rest of the Church. It would
> also revive the notion of servant leadership, in which the minister-
> ial task of the pope would be to encourage the growth of subsidiar-
> ity through which the local church would assume more
> responsibility for living out the faith in its own area. It would be

part of the gradual abandonment of the monarchical and bureaucratic centralism that at present characterises Roman attitudes.

(Collins, 1997)

How probable is such a development?

Part of the problem is the unresolved tension between the outcomes of the First and Second Vatican Councils and in the ambiguities inherent in the teachings of the latter. Vatican I defined the
jurisdictional primacy of the Pope over the whole Church reinforced
by the declaration of infallibility. Vatican II reaffirmed this teaching but placed the idea of the People of God, sharing a fundamental
dignity and baptismal equality, at the centre of its 'Constitution on
the Church' before considerations of hierarchy as service. The
teaching on episcopal office was developed and the New Testament
emphasis on collegiality was reclaimed and affirmed. Fr Cosgrave
summarizes the implications as follows:

> the Council discussed collegiality as pertaining largely to the
> papal–episcopal level, and while open to it at all levels, e.g.
> bishop and priests, priests and laity, it was not as clear and un-
> equivocal about these other levels as one might have wished . . .
> since *Lumen Gentium* is in important ways a compromise
> document, as between the more conservative and the more pro-
> gressive bishops at the Council, it is open to being quoted selec-
> tively . . . the fact of a real polarisation is indisputable. This
> division is based ultimately on theological differences, rooted
> in contrasting ecclesiologies and, in particular, in differing
> theologies of authority . . . and how it should be understood, struc-
> tured and used.

(Cosgrave, 1996)

Despite a number of developments intended to enhance the authority of the college of bishops since Vatican II, Gaillardetz suggests
that real impediments exist to the full and proper exercise of its
authority. The potentialities of local episcopal conferences and the
world synod of bishops have not been realized. Notwithstanding
recent attempts at reform, the college of cardinals – a medieval in-
vention – has largely co-opted the divinely instituted authority of
the college of bishops which Gaillardetz believes results in

> a system of governance that marginalizes the college of bishops,
> undermines a real exercise of collegiality, and consequently di-
> minishes the ecclesiological significance of the life of the local
> church as a contribution to the church universal.

(1997)

The Roman Curia also remain unreformed, contrary to the wishes of the Council. Neither the Council nor the revised Code of Canon Law satisfactorily resolved 'the thorny complex of canonical and ecclesiological questions regarding the function and authority of the Roman curia'. The doctrinal teaching authority of the Pope (as bishop of Rome) cannot be delegated. Yet, the distinction between the legislative functions of the Pope and the bishops and the executive role of the Curia has been ignored with the result, Gaillardetz maintains, that 'the congregations of the Roman curia have virtually replaced the college of bishops as the principal legislators of the church'. This development has been compounded, in his view, by widespread ignorance of the difference between documents issued in 'common' form (carrying general papal endorsement) and those promulgated in 'special' form, which the Pope had made his own. This confusion has lent 'an authority to curial documents that may be unwarranted ecclesiologically'. Gaillardetz concludes that

> A reinvigoration of Vatican II's vision of episcopal collegiality and an ecclesiology of communion cannot occur without a fundamental shift of responsibility for assisting the pope in the pastoral care of the universal church back to the college of bishops where, *according to church teaching*, it belongs.

The situation cries out for resolution through the bishops claiming their God-given authority and, if necessary, insisting upon a third Council to give institutional effect to reform.

SUPPRESSION OF VARIETY AND THE TREATMENT OF THEOLOGICAL DISSENT

The present centralizing tendencies of the papacy clearly limit the freedom and effectiveness of the local church. This can be illustrated using an analogy from cybernetics. Ashby's so-called 'law of requisite variety' (1956) suggests that a systems controller must have available to him or her at least as much variety in response as is likely to appear at any time in the system to be controlled. Governments, including church government, lack such variety of response and consequently react by trying to reduce variety in the system to manageable proportions with consequent frustration and resentment at local level. We see this manifested in regulations, directives, the codifying of canon law and the manifold problems of inculturation. At the same time, participatory initiatives at parish and diocesan level are increasing system complexity and variety; a consequence of the unresolved and contradictory tensions at the Second Vatican Council.

The following examples illustrate some of the difficulties.

• Archbishop Quinn in his centennial lecture at Campion Hall noted that the Second Vatican Council lacked 'sufficient appreciation of the great cultural diversity in the church' when it pronounced the Roman rite with its 'hieratic measured gravity' normative for the Latin Church. In similar vein, Bishop Clark (1997) asks 'why cannot an episcopal conference apply the teachings of the gospel to the concrete situation of their own nations or region without the intervention of others who are unfamiliar with that concrete situation?'

• In their 1977 *'Statement Concerning the Revision of the Code of Canon Law'*, the Canon Law Society of America pointed out that 'the Church today lives within various juridical cultures. Roman Catholics from one culture (e.g. the 'Common Law' tradition) find it difficult to be heard or understood by persons from a different legal culture (e.g. the 'Civil Law' tradition). Without a very deliberate effort, which does not appear to be happening, communication over very basic legal issues becomes confused and misunderstanding results'.

• Again, from a Third World perspective, Fr Aloysius Pieris has suggested that 'The cloud of incomprehension that surrounded recent discussions on liberation theology in the official churches in the West cannot be dispelled fully without realising that the two parties in dispute were using two theological languages, albeit within the same orthodox Christian tradition' (two paradigms which) 'differ primarily in the way they combine the secular-humanist and the biblical-religious components of their respective theologies'. He argues that 'certain First World theologians tend to universalise and absolutise their paradigm, unmindful of its contextual particularity and ideological limitations', resulting in a tendency towards ecclesiastical imperialism. He cites human rights theology 'ideologically tied to the Western model of social organisation' as a case in point. He suggests that its 'imposition' violates the autonomy of the local church and he appeals to the Western patriarchate, 'Even in the struggle for justice, let justice be done to the creativity of the Third World Religions.'

• More specifically, from the point of view of one local church, Fr Felix Wilfred of Madras University describes the typical Indian perception of the Catholic Church. It is seen, he suggests, as a

powerful and wealthy international institution which expanded
under the influence of colonial rule. It is not only alien to the culture of the people but predominantly negative and hostile in its
judgement of their religious heritage which, at best, is to be 'fulfilled and crowned by the Christian dispensation'. The foreign
missionaries of the colonial period were engrossed in the work of
conversion and did not promote serious theological reflection,
nor was the general atmosphere conducive to it.

> The theological content and method followed in India and
> imparted to the candidates to priesthood were divorced
> from the concrete socio-political realities of the people. The
> imported theology of Scholastic and Enlightenment stamp
> was concerned more about the elucidations of universal and
> 'perennial' concepts than with the life-realities of the people
> and their historical context . . . The new generation of indi-
> genous leaders schooled as they were in Western theological
> tradition, and moulded by colonial values, tastes, thought-
> patterns, and way of life, simply continued the theological
> path of their missionary-mentors . . . The situation has not
> changed in any appreciable way even today . . . There is a
> close connection between the quality of theological thinking
> and the mode of the exercise of authority in the Church.
> Where orthodoxy, power and control become the over-
> arching concern, theological thinking is atrophied . . . In
> this respect, the fresh and bold ventures seen among our
> brothers and sisters of other Christian denominations in
> India, was not to be found in the Indian Catholic theological
> tradition until very recent times. To this we should add also
> the clericalism and centralisation of thought that has charac-
> terised the life of the Church.
>
>   (Wilfred, 1994)

- Closer to home, Ryan (1996) suggests that the Catholic Church's
  culture of internal control is, in part, a response to the reverses
  suffered by the Church in the nineteenth century; an organizational regression damaging to the intellectual and moral consciousness of the laity and the understanding of what it means to
  be Christian. He reflects that the Church appears more afraid to
  change than to die. Yet, at the same time, his study of contemporary Midlands parishes reveals a gradual process of responsive
  adaptation, involving delegation of responsibility to the laity,
  new roles for religious, and a hunger for spiritual direction. The
  process is, nevertheless, limited, he suggests, by a number of

factors including: the persistence of pre-Vatican II models of priesthood among some priests; the immature faith and low levels of commitment among many Catholics which inhibits the best efforts of priests to involve them; and an inability to understand, communicate effectively with and motivate young people – the two-universes problem. Significantly, from a systems perspective, he notes that the absence of developed feedback mechanisms in the Church means that the lessons of Vatican II are not being absorbed and acted upon organizationally. The pastoral insights and richness of local initiatives are lost without structural adaptation to increase variety in systems response.

We see the lack of 'requisite variety' also in the limitations placed on more general freedom in theological enquiry. Commenting upon the 1990 'Instruction on the Ecclesial Vocation of the Theologian', Collins (1997) suggests that the Instruction explicitly denies that there is a theological magisterium and conflates the papal magisterium and the curial 'magisterium' (both equally binding on theologians and believers). 'The papacy alone is the judge of theological truth.'

Contrasting the century-old practice, prior to Vatican II, of popes and bishops consulting exclusively 'court theologians' with the subsequent expectations that the International Theological Commission created by Pope Paul VI would engage internationally respected theologians of differing views in discussion with the Holy See (including the Congregation for the Doctrine of the Faith), Gaillardetz expresses disappointment:

> A frequent consultation of theologians representing divergent views on a matter need not threaten the legitimate authority of those who hold Church Office. Unfortunately, in the last fifteen years the diversity of views represented by the ITC membership has diminished considerably and some fear a return to the practice of limiting consultation to 'court theologians'.
>
> (Gaillardetz, 1997)

Informed commentators and ordinary lay people alike express concern at the treatment of theologians disciplined for their opinions apparently without due process and in seeming contradiction to the Church's public statements on justice and human rights. Fr Reese indicates that

> those who have been subjected to the process object that it is flawed. They say that the accusations brought against the accused are sometimes vague; there is a failure to distinguish

between dogma and theological opinion; only experts agreeing
with the Vatican are consulted; the reporter for the author is not
chosen by the author; and the theologian is not notified of an investigation until after the congregation has concluded that
errors are present.

(Reese, 1996)

This suggests that

The relationship between theologians and the papacy is worse
today than at any time since the Reformation. The number of
theologians investigated, silenced, or removed from office is at
an all-time high, even exceeding the numbers during the Modernist crisis at the beginning of this century. The rhetoric used by
theologians in response to Vatican actions has been bitter and
biting. The chasm between the two appears to be getting wider,
not narrower. A breach between the intellectual and administrative leaders of an organisation is, of course, a recipe for disaster.

(Reese, 1996)

New regulations governing the process of investigation were published in August 1997. Designed to take account of criticisms of the
procedures adopted by the Congregation for the Doctrine of the
Faith since 1971, they are intended to offer additional safeguards
to theologians whose work comes under scrutiny. The safeguards
permit the author's bishop to act as an intermediary and the advo-
cate, appointed by the CDF, to take a more active role in interpreting the teachings concerned and in stressing their positive aspects.
The author may also nominate an adviser to appear with him and
assist him. Neither the bishop nor the adviser may be present,
however, when decisions are taken.

BOUNDARIES OF ORTHODOXY

As a consequence of centralization and fear, the boundaries of
orthodoxy appear to be drawn ever tighter. Fr O'Brien describes
the situation as follows:

The overriding concern of the church universal at the moment
seems to be a pre-occupation with Catholic identity – ever more
narrowly defined ... The code word for this, first enunciated by
Cardinal Ratzinger, and the real agenda, is 'the restoration of
pre-Vatican II values' ... The institutional face of the church is
relentlessly organising itself in pursuit of these goals and its

system of recruitment, appointments, expenditure and communication is ample evidence of this.

(O'Brien, 1994)

Committed but 'unorthodox' Catholics feel themselves being defined out of the Church and are faced with agonizing decisions about disengagement. Some leave (many younger ones never make a real commitment to join in the first place), others redefine the nature of their spiritual lives and endeavour to live out their Christian vocation outside the redrawn boundaries, crossing the boundary for (minimal) eucharistic nourishment. Those who come forward for instruction – for example through RCIA – are not infrequently prevented from completing the process because of their family circumstances, previous relationships or current difficulties. The problems may admit of no easily foreseeable resolution. The outcome may be experienced as rejection; at best it is painful for those involved. Questions of orthodoxy make their deepest impression when they touch upon people's intimate personal lives. Here the gap between teaching and sensitive pastoral practice is widest.

It is frequently people's experience of relationship with the local priest and his way of mediating church teaching that is crucial. In some cases the priest, in touch with pastoral realities in a way which his superiors are not, ignores or gets around the regulations. The accounts of inter-church families testify to the emotional release and deep impact on their spiritual lives that such humane and pastorally sensitive decisions may have. On the other hand, relationships between priest and people may be problematic, especially with women. The difficulty is increasingly recognized but the socialization of priests into the culture of the Church creates problems. This leads to questions about priestly formation, the nature of ministerial priesthood and its relationship to the priesthood of all baptized people. Are comparisons with the early Church a help or a hindrance here? How do people *really* feel about collaborative ministry and how might it work in practice?

CONSTRAINTS ON COLLABORATION

Drawing attention to the trend towards consultation and collaboration in civic, social and working life, the accompanying changes in management style and the implications for the 'classic' dependency model of parish organization, Fr Cooper (1993) pointed out:

We are currently witnessing the abandonment of old hierarchical structures in which a chosen elite exercise all the power, to more diverse and collaborative forms of organisation in which a greater number of employees share power. This change poses certain problems for the church, since many clergy, though willing to sacrifice their status, lack the vision and skills to initiate collaboration with their lay colleagues ... many were trained in the dynamics of one-on-one ministry and lack the necessary skills to engage effectively in group process that forms the foundation for collaborative ministry.

Nor was he optimistic about current programmes of priestly formation:

How can seminarians identify and develop the necessary skills to be effective in collaborative ministry when the courses required to refine these skills are not currently offered. My concern is that we are currently training a new generation of clergy who have the right jargon, but lack the basic skills necessary for exercising effective leadership in the church. An urgent need is to provide all ordained ministers with a comprehensive formation program in group process that is inclusive of lay ministers.

Fr Cooper emphasized that

This style of collegiate leadership calls everyone to a different level of maturity and communion. Collaboration in ministry demands a greater depth of self-awareness, in that it calls for a level of co-operation that is less dependent, more self-revealing and demands a commitment to emotional honesty and the willingness to deal with conflict in a mature way. A collaborative vision of ministry perceives authority as the creative capacity to call forth the vision and gifts of others. In this context authority invites rather than controls, nurtures rather than constricts.

(Cooper, 1993)

Is it reasonable to expect greater enthusiasm from an ageing, apparently ill-prepared and arguably overburdened population of priests (more than 60 per cent of whom are over 50 years old in Great Britain) for the personally challenging and painful transformation in ministerial style entailed?

A DIMINISHED AND DISORIENTED PRIESTHOOD

Fr O'Brien (1994), reflecting upon the excessive demands upon priests striving to fulfil their leadership roles and meet the expectations of their parishioners in the Irish church, suggests:

It is amazing that so many managed to fill such a role for so long ... Inexorably, priests became involved in a series of contemporaneous power struggles with a wide variety of interest groups; struggles they were bound to lose, given the kind of society which had emerged ... In the meantime, there is a sense of diminution and disorientation. The traditional role has become impossible ... the malaise is evident when priests gather to talk. We might distinguish three kinds of conversation. There are those who will talk about anything under the sun except theology and the faith itself. In some cases, this is because of a fear of what it might open up; in others, it is because of an apparently rock-like certainty that the faith and the church are so permanent and unchanging that exploration of any kind is irrelevant.

For a second group, there is talk of the church and things theological, but all with a somewhat painful air of negativity. Whether it is nostalgia for the past, anger at powerlessness, confusion about where to turn or criticism that will never lead to action, these conversations, far from focusing and empowering the participants, send them away even more depressed.

A third group wants change, eagerly discusses pastoral initiatives as well as their theological premises, but for the most part experiences a solid wall of incomprehension and opposition from those with the power to make decisions. Some just get on with the job, free themselves from dependence on approval and try to be creative. For others, the predominant experience is that of observing the disorientation of the church being compounded by the refusal to change. For a minority, there is the good fortune of actually obtaining permission and sometimes even support for their initiatives.

... But the laity is hurting too, because this sense of dislocation and creeping irrelevance produces a lack of leadership and an uncertain, if not to say non-existent, pastoral strategy. This result is a perfunctory pastoral performance, trite homilies, boring liturgies, minimal visitation and the absence of a social project. In the search for relevance, the conventional is canonised. Soon we are merely repeating what the world has already said sooner and – on its own terms at least – more effectively.

(O'Brien, 1994)

AN IMMATURE AND DIVIDED PEOPLE?

As previously noted by Ryan (1996), the reality of parish life as experienced by many priests in the Midlands is of a people, competent in other aspects of life, who behave like children in the Church, are ignorant about the faith, must be asked to become involved and require constant supervision. The reason, he suggests, for the inability of many Catholics to exercise their gifts within the Church is precisely that the capacity was never developed because it was never intended to be used. He maintains that the 'militarized' model of defensive church inherited from the nineteenth century was not relational, and priestly formation did not develop relational capacity. It emphasized the apartness of the Catholic community and sought to provide both a Catholic identity through the Catholic school and a complete life world (whereas now more than two-thirds of Catholics marry a partner who is not a Catholic). Authoritarianism backed by social control reduced faith to dogma mediated through educational and catechetical structures frequently experienced as oppressive. Formulas governed behaviour. Obligations (principally Mass attendance) were emphasized but discharged without understanding. Behaviour that should have been a free and loving response to the gospel could be achieved more speedily − if uncomprehendingly − through moral pressure and social control. Responsibilities were highly regulated, therefore immaturity was normative. Clerical monopoly of control produced lay reluctance to exercise initiative; a sacramentalized, catechized, moralized but not evangelized people. Priests now report the paralysing consequences of institutional power exercised in the interests of such conformity and obedience.

> As more priests try to build the relationships upon which ministries and enablement depend, they find that the ghost of the old model of priesthood needs exorcising no less than the old model of parish . . . Taking him out of his own community, making him a man apart, and then returning him to a community not his own as a formal role-player rather than a builder of relationships meant that he became a role-model only for a narrow idea of priesthood, not for community life at large. He could be a model for chastity but with difficulty for generosity; for loyalty and obedience but rarely for mature, other-regarding independence.
>
> (Ryan, 1996)

In contrast, the testimonies of the minority of active Catholics supplied to the Queens Working Party tell rather a different story. They reveal widespread pain and frustration as a result of the prevailing institutional culture which, despite the best efforts of good and generous priests and bishops, is nevertheless experienced as predominantly autocratic, inflexible, lacking in humanity, fearful of change. Women, especially, find clerical attitudes hard to bear. Interchurch families speak movingly of the obstacles they face in living a full Christian life in the context of the regulations governing the sacraments.

Further, the Church often does not exemplify in its internal practice the values which it proclaims in its social teaching. Inefficiency, lack of professionalism, poor management and financial controls can cost the Catholic community dear. Abrupt changes of policy at the whim of incoming parish priests (which may be backed by reference to canon law), coupled with poor job security, suggest that lay pastoral workers are frequently regarded as dispensable with consequent loss of self-esteem and, for paid workers, financial hardship. They are expected to bear the economic and emotional cost without complaint or recourse to the civil law out of loyalty to the Church. Others may leave voluntarily, lacking affirmation, tired of the uphill struggle to influence events, offer leadership or exercise their gifts.

Whether active or passive, committed to what Fr Hill (1988) terms 'magisterial papalist' or 'ministerial collegialist' visions of the Church, the challenge for both lay and ordained members is to live and act in a spirit of charity, through the uncertainty, the tension and the complexity which accompanies the institutional response to contemporary culture. The signs, however, point not so much to generosity of spirit towards those with opposing points of view as, in some cases, to latent hostility and polarization. Thus, in August 1996 Cardinal Bernardin launched the 'Common Ground' initiative in the United States to 'move beyond the distrust, the polarization, and the entrenched positions' that have hampered the American church in its ability to 'address, creatively and faithfully questions that are vital if the Church in the United States is to flourish as we enter the next millennium'. This search for common ground must, he said, be 'Centred on faith in Jesus, marked by accountability to the living catholic tradition and ruled by a new spirit of civility, dialogue, generosity and a broad and serious consultation'. Sadly, since the Cardinal's death, anecdotal evidence points to a hardening of positions with ecclesiastical backing.

In the UK, such polarization has not occurred, but the English bishops, nevertheless, speak with growing concern about the destructive influence of right-wing groups in the Church, their abusive and sometimes vicious attacks on the integrity of individuals and the fact that their faces are set against dialogue or openness to rational discussion. The radical groups, on the other hand, are open to persuasive argument and are easier to deal with, though they occasionally delight – as one bishop put it – in acting like naughty children. Fr Reese suggests that, among reformist Catholics,

> More recently, organised dissent has moved beyond the theological community with large-scale petition drives netting millions of signatures in Germany, Austria, Belgium, and Italy. If this movement spreads, internal church conflict and anticlericalism will increase unless church leaders find a way of responding positively to the issues. There is always a danger of a schism on the left matching Archbishop Lefebvre's schism on the right, although such a threat is not imminent. The more likely response will be the withdrawal from active participation by Catholic elites alienated from the hierarchy or by ordinary Catholics upset by bickering within the church.
>
> (Reese, 1996)

Lay Participation

In practice, it is not untypical to live all one's live within the same diocese without ever being asked one's opinion on any matter of diocesan or even parish significance. Sadly, people are so unused to being asked that they are a bit cynical when genuine attempts at consultation do occur – or so it appears. There is talk of regional synods and diocesan synods and some experience of both. There are diocesan pastoral councils and many parish councils – but the majority of such pieces of machinery pass most people by. In England, *Easter People*, the National Pastoral Congress and the celebrations of the Church's social teaching have not been followed up. An important reason for this, apparently, is Rome's fear of anything that smacks of parliamentary procedure within the national church.

The experience of government in other denominations is valuable, but the Catholic bishops appear to regard the lessons in a somewhat negative light. What they see as the politics and bureaucracy of the Church of England synod structure and the methods of settling questions of authority in the Church of Scotland leave many bishops grateful that they are free of such structures. Part of their reluctance to embrace comparable structures with significant lay involvement may, of course, have something to do with the limitations it would impose upon their freedom. Representatives of other denominations writing on the subject acknowledge the difficulties. The assemblies tend to be dominated by middle-aged, middle-class males with consequent implications. There is too great an emphasis upon 'winning' the debate and too hasty a willingness to act upon majority decisions rather than to convince minorities. Inevitably, lobby groups attempt to influence outcomes – with accompanying strife and manoeuvring for roles. The structures can prove large and unwieldy; the agendas too full for careful and informed decision-making. The investment of time (typically during working hours) imposes heavy demands upon those involved, particularly in certain areas, and limits the field of candidates. Yet, participants remain largely supportive. Canon Martin Reardon, retired General Secretary of Churches Together in England, professionally engaged in the Church of England Synod and an observer of other churches' structures of government, comments in a letter to the author that, on balance, his 'experience has been largely positive – particularly of the way the Methodist Church builds up a remarkable corporate identity, and the way the Church of England is synodically governed and episcopally led'. He suggests that a survey of church structures in England might be helpful to the Catholic bishops and points to the danger that ignorance about representative Catholic opinion on controversial issues may lead to lack of episcopal adventure. Greater lay participation in the Catholic Church presupposes a change in the underlying psychological model described by Dominian and in the levels of maturity and appetite for active pastoral involvement among ordinary parishioners. It also demands a radical review of resource allocations to give significantly greater priority to adult religious formation compared to other expenditures.

Examples of good practice from other large international institutions might also prove illuminating, but it seems that appropriate studies are yet to appear, though Terry Connor and Sarah Lindsell suggest that, as a voluntary organization itself, the Church shares many of the characteristics of the secular voluntary movement and would benefit from the insights, experiences and organizational models developed within the voluntary sector.

APPOINTMENTS

Lay people at present have little influence on the selection of those going forward to train as priests, let alone influence over the choice of their parish priest or bishop. Though, as both Duffy and Gaillardetz remind us, current practice is relatively modern and canon law makes provision for local election of bishops. There are anxieties about the quality of candidates for the priesthood, for example, their sexual orientation, their frequently disturbed family backgrounds, relatively conservative attitudes and so on. The overwhelming majority of Catholics are heterosexual – what are the implications of a ministerial priesthood which does not reflect the sexual orientation of the population of believers? What are the implications for relational authority of a priesthood in which the proportion of damaged personalities appears to be significantly higher than among the population of believers, especially given the emphasis in canon law on their competence to govern? Leaving aside the vexed question of women's ordination, competent adult males, married and unmarried (*viri probati*), exist who could be approached – for example, active, retired men with occupational pensions are available in increasing numbers (some formerly ordained). This might remove opposition on economic grounds which, church leaders admit, is probably the main constraint. Consultation procedures over appointments are criticized as a waste of time by some (including bishops). This may be so if people are unformed and uninformed; not prepared carefully; ignorant of the criteria for appointment or the profile and requirements of the sought-for candidate, and not confident that their opinions will be treated seriously. The Pope is of the opinion that no priest should be forced to become a bishop. Nor, according to the old canon law principle 'that what touches all should be approved by all', should priests be made bishops who do not have the approbation of the people. Priests, it seems, are not always asked the question in a way which leaves them free – rather, the invitation may come from the nuncio in the form of a personal request from the Pope. Some apparently would have refused the appointment, had the context been such that they felt free to do so.

Gaillardetz (1997) suggests that 'No ecclesiastical practice exerts a more significant influence on the life of the local church than the manner in which bishops are appointed ... The circumvention of the real participation of the whole community in the appointment of a bishop can impair that reciprocal relationship' which characterizes the ministry of a bishop. That is, bringing the faith to the people and bearing back to the universal Church the witness, experience and celebration of that faith. Many appointments of bishops are, no doubt, in accordance with the wishes of the local church. Others are not. As McRedmond (1995) indicates, the result has been that, in recent years, the local church has been divided, alienated and angered by the choice. 'Bewilderment, pain and a sense of outrage' has, he reports, marked the reaction to appointments in the Netherlands in the 1970s, Austria in the 1980s, Switzerland, the Philippines and Latin America in the 1990s. Norway is a recent addition to the latter group of unhappy choices.

McRedmond questions the pivotal role of the nuncio in such appointments in contrast to the wishes of the local church. Contrary to the vision of the council fathers, the bishop becomes a visible foundation of disunity when his appointment 'is seen to be a cause of dissension, protest, alienation of clergy or laity or both'.

Bishop Clark argues for a return to an election process which includes the whole Church in open and prayerful discernment, 'a vast improvement over the present process of secret individual consultations'. Such a process would be consistent with the principle of subsidiarity and with the call of the entire people of God, by Vatican II, to responsibility for the mission of the Church. Bishop Clark acknowledges that politics may enter into the process but argues that politics 'will be subject to moderation by public scrutiny'.

Acknowledging the half-truth in what McRedmond terms the irrelevant and tiresome assertion that the Church is not a democracy, Gaillardetz (1997) argues that

> Local participation in episcopal appointments should not be identified with that understanding of election that has its roots in political liberalism ... The understanding of 'election' in political liberalism is that of an aggregate polling of individual preferences. However, an ecclesiological commitment to local participation of the faithful in the election of a bishop requires a different dynamic. The people of God submit themselves to the guidance of the Spirit in a process of corporate discernment that is intent upon serving the will of God in the community's corporate choice of a candidate ... Anyone aware of Church history knows that the Spirit is able to work in the midst of sometimes scandalous manifestations of political infighting and intrigue.
>
> The election of the bishop by the local community is an alternative means of episcopal selection that may reflect the democratic tendencies of our modern age, but much more, it is a practice in keeping with our most ancient ecclesial insights regarding the bishop's immersion within the local believing community.

(Gaillardetz, 1997)

The uncertainty surrounding the extent to which the present imbalances in power between Rome and the local church on the one hand, and priests and people on the other, can or will be redressed in the years to come, makes it difficult to propose realistic and helpful suggestions about increased participation and involvement of lay people in the decisions which affect their lives. Participation is, in any event, constrained by canon law, as Fr Ombres points out in the present volume.

Mgr Hypher reminds us that, according to the Second Vatican Council, 'the parish must be a place of discussion and discernment about the critical issues facing its members and facing the world'. Quoting Dr Ryan (1996), he suggests that if 'the failure of the structures of the Church to match even its own stated objectives is a failure of *organisational process*, then this failure plainly also constitutes a failure of the structures of authority, certainly at diocesan and parish level'. Referring to the revised Code of Canon Law, he notes that,

> At the same time, therefore, as striving to protect the priest's established authority, the Code also seeks to assert the baptismal rights and responsibilities of the lay faithful ... These two positions are frankly contradictory and the Code seems to be blind to the consequences of having such an inbuilt imbalance between the juridical rights of the priest on the one hand and the obligations with no juridical status attached which belong to the laity on the other.
>
> What the Church seems to fail to recognise is that such a juxtaposition of incompatible statements is not only inefficient, it is thoroughly destructive.
>
> (Hypher, 1997)

Fortunately, Fr Orsy offers some grounds for optimism in relation to the Code's denial of powers of jurisdiction to lay persons:

> The content of this canon is no more than a respectable opinion ... It cannot be upheld on historical grounds. Lay persons, among them women abbesses with quasi-episcopal power, possessed with the consent and co-operation of the Holy See power that corresponded in every way to the description of jurisdiction.
>
> (Orsy, 1997)

Structural Change

The bishops are careful to emphasize that Pope John Paul II himself is an open and attentive listener, that he thinks in collborative terms, is typically well briefed and keen to understand the local pastoral situation. Yet, as Archbishop Quinn has pointed out, collaboration is not the full measure of collegiality. Bishops also have a responsibility, with the Pope, for confronting the problems and possibilities for the mission of the Church. This requires reform of the central government of the Church; a process hindered by the attitude of the Curia and the machinery of government. Many bishops are concerned about the way the Curia attempts to control communications at synods, at the success of Vatican officials with no pastoral responsibilities in curtailing certain topics of discussion, and so on. Thus, Bishop Clark asks

> How can the college of bishops under the presidency of the bishop of Rome be said to govern the universal Church when decisions about the content of the deposit of faith are attributed to them without careful and thorough consultation? As true vicars of Christ who represent the Great Church to the local church, how can they be asked credibly to defend among their people policies to which they have not contributed and texts which they have never seen?
>
> (Clark, 1997)

In his 1996 Campion Hall lecture, Archbishop Quinn offered a frank and sensitive analysis of many features of the central government of the Church. He paid tribute to the dedication, professionalism and holiness of many of those involved but acknowledged that others did not share those qualities. He noted Cardinal Yves Congar's view that personal holiness, of itself, is insufficient to bring about change and endorsed his conclusion that reform of the papacy must extend beyond attitudinal change to embrace structures. Cardinal Congar believed that, despite the thirst for reform in the Middle Ages, attention focused on specific abuses and consequently the men and women of the age 'missed their rendezvous with opportunity'.

> Most of those who wanted reform, he said, were prisoners of the system, incapable of reforming the structures themselves through a recovery of the original vision, incapable of asking the new questions raised by a new situation. Reform meant to them simply putting the existing structures in order. The further, deeper, long-term questions were never asked. Their vision stopped at the water's edge. The moment passed, and a wounded Church suffered incomparable tragedy.
>
> (Congar, quoted in Quinn, 1996)

Archbishop Quinn indicated that many Christians are hesitant about full communion with Rome, not principally because of historical or doctrinal reasons but because of the way in which issues are dealt with by the Curia. Such concern is worldwide:

> The importance of a major structural reform of the Curia cannot be underestimated. After the internationalization effected by

Paul VI and the rearrangement of some competencies, the reforms which have taken place since have been relatively minor and have been designed by members of the Curia itself. The major change of outlook and structural reform which 'the new situation' requires would ideally be the work of a broader constituency. A commission, for example, could be created with three presidents. One, a representative of an episcopal conference, one, a representative of the Curia and the third, a lay person.

(Quinn, 1996)

Such a working commission should, he suggests, consult widely and report within three years. The plan should be presented to the presidents of episcopal conferences for a vote and to the Pope for approval and implementation.

Fr Hill argues from a *ministerial collegialist* perspective and suggests

turning the triennial synod of bishops into a genuinely deliberative body, converting the Roman curia into a network of purely advisory and consultative organisations, and discontinuing the curial appointment of nearly all the bishops. In particular bishops' conferences should be seen as a modern revival of the ancient synodal form of church government, and recognised as being the most proper bodies for making decisions and laws and policies best suited to the needs and circumstances of the local churches in their areas. It should be for them to decide, for example, whether or not to ordain married men; how and on what conditions people may be dispensed from the ordained ministry. It should be for them to make the final decisions about liturgy, about marriage customs, dispensations, etc., and about other points of Church discipline.

It is to be hoped that they would appreciate, not simply the value, but the necessity of admitting to their counsels representatives of the clergy, the laity and the religious (women as well as men).

... What I am in fact proposing is the 'planned dissolution' of the Latin Church into a considerable number of distinct, autonomous 'patriarchates' – not necessarily each with a patriarch, but each with quite as much autonomy as the ancient Eastern patriarchates now enjoy ... Over all the other Churches the Church of Rome would continue to preside in charity, and its bishop, the pope, to exercise a purely Petrine, and no longer a patriarchal authority ... Authority is a necessary safeguard, but the less it has to be exercised, the better. Let the Baptist's words, Jn 3:30, always be their motto: 'he must increase, but I must decrease'.

(Hill, 1988)

Fr Reese also favours subsidiarity as a guiding principle of reform, with greater local inculturation and experimentation. It would, he feels, also make unity with other churches easier to negotiate. He further suggests:

> To respond to the needs of a communion of churches, the curia might be reorganised on geographical lines rather than the current mix of geography, issues, and constituencies. There could be five offices, one for each continent (Africa, Asia, Europe, North America, and Latin America), that would handle the appointment of bishops and relations with the local churches in each region. A curia organised by geographical regions might more easily implement the principle of subsidiarity in the church. Such a structure is likely to be more sensitive to the need to inculturate Christianity in local contexts, with less concern for uniformity around the world. Under this model, there could be interdicasterial committees to co-ordinate policy toward seminaries, clergy, laity, religious, liturgy, doctrine, and finances in different regions of the world. But the institutional thrust would be toward inculturation rather than uniformity.

(Reese, 1996)

Finally, both Reese (1996) and Collins (1997) propose regular *ecumenical* councils (e.g. every 25 years) 'so that each generation of bishops could share experiences, reflect on the state of the church, and take actions necessary to respond to a rapidly changing cultural environment'. Collins, however, would prefer to see a *'general council'* first:

> What we need first is a *general* rather than an *ecumenical* council. This distinction is very useful here. A general council (like the councils of this millennium) represents the Western Roman Catholic Church: an ecumenical council is much broader, and includes representatives of all Christians. If there were regular decennial general councils these could gradually move toward a universal and truly ecumenical council. This would happen with the increasingly full participation of the Orthodox, Protestants, and Anglicans. In fact, a genuine reform of the papacy could open the way to the ecumenical Christian Church of the future.

(Collins, 1997)

Conclusion

Lumen Gentium defined the Church as the community of disciples of Christ sharing a fundamental baptismal equality and personal dignity. All members of the Church are called to full and active participation in the life of the Church in the service of God's people and the fulfilment of their baptismal vocation. In the foregoing pages, I have tried to describe the many difficulties that currently limit full participation in the Church. Taken in isolation, many of these might perhaps be considered as instances of institutional inflexibility and inertia, which in time, with moderate good will and a willingness to adapt, will result in appropriate structural adjustments. Sadly, when taken together, they suggest a far more serious, painful and disturbing conclusion: institutional error, injustice and, conscious or unconscious, an apparent abuse of power by many of those in authority. These deficiencies must be confronted – in charity – but confronted nonetheless if the fruits of Vatican II – what Pope John Paul II in 1994 termed the 'great gift of the Spirit to the church at the end of the second millennium' – are to be realized.

In preparation for the 'Great Jubilee' the Pope has invited Christians to an examination of conscience, the promotion of 'fitting ecumenical initiatives' and consideration of the reception given to Vatican II. He also enquired whether the ecclesiology of communion in *Lumen Gentium* is being strengthened and warned against 'adopting notions borrowed from democracy and sociology which do not reflect the vision of the church and the authentic spirit of Vatican II'.

Quoting the above sections of *Tertio Millennio Adveniente*, Gaillardetz remarks:

> In his apostolic letter the pope was careful to avoid calling the Catholic Church *qua* Church to this kind of examination of conscience. Sinfulness and error were only attributed to the 'sons and daughters' of the Church. But surely the examination of conscience he called for must have a corporate and ecclesial dimension. It must be legitimate to ask how we can, *as a Church*, in preparation for the coming millennium, strengthen the ecclesiology of communion and further the cause of Christian unity. As I noted in the introduction, this call for an examination of conscience was given a new specificity in the Pope's encyclical on ecumenism, in which he called for further study regarding the nature of teaching authority in the Church.
>
> (Gaillardetz, 1997)

Fr Kelly suggests that

> for Christians 'sin' is fundamentally a positive word. Its Christian meaning is inextricably bound up with our belief in a God of healing and forgiveness. Hence, the very 'owning' of one's sinfulness (and sin) before God is a transformative act. It is the first step on the road to conversion.
>
> ... To speak of sin with regard to office-holders in the Church is to acknowledge their solidarity with the rest of us. Unlike what we say of Christ in the Fourth Eucharistic Prayer, they are like us in all things, including sin. To make sin a taboo word in speaking of them is to refuse to face human reality. It also shows a lack of faith in the power of God's healing spirit active in the Church – and a lack of faith in the office-holders in question to be open to that Spirit ... The ultimate object of faith is God. God is the one in whom we believe. To believe in the Church is to believe in God acting in and through the Church. To borrow a phrase from Rahner, the Holy Spirit is the dynamic element in the Church. That is why it is totally inadequate to interpret 'we believe in a Church of sinners' as meaning 'we believe in a Church in which, on balance, there is more good than evil'. Our belief in the Church is not a judgement of proportionality. It is belief in the living presence and action of God in the Church. That is why any pessimism or fatalism with regard to the Church must be 'disowned' as unchristian. It stands in contradiction to belief in the Church.

(Kelly, 1993)

With the prayerful support of the wider Christian community, the Millennium provides a unique opportunity for those in authority in the Church, both to lead and to engage in the personal and institutional examination of conscience which Fr Kelly and Gaillardetz propose. A willingness to 'own' and confront the institutional sinfulness that would emerge from such an enquiry would do much to build confidence in the Church and provide the 'inspiration of the whole of Christian living' which Pope John Paul II is seeking.

References

Ahrendt, D. and Young, K. (1994) 'Authoritarianism Updated', in Roger Jowel et al. (eds), *British Social Attitudes, the 11th Report*, Aldershot: Dartmouth Publishing.

Alford, H. (1996) 'Reflections on the Centenary of the Bushey Congregation of Sisters', New Blackfriars, 77(906).

Ashby, W. R. (1956) *Introduction to Cybernetics*, New York: Wiley.

Barker, D. (1993) 'Values and Volunteering', in J. Davis Smith (ed.), *Volunteering in Europe: Opportunities and Challenges for the 90's*, Berkhamsted: The Volunteer Centre.

Barker, D., Halman, L. and Vloet, A. (1992) *The European Values Study 1981–1990 Summary Report*, Aberdeen: The Gordon Cook Foundation.

Bingemer, M. C. (1989) 'Women in the Future of the Theology of Liberation', in Marc H. Ellis and Otto Meduro (eds), *The Future of Liberation Theology: Essays in Honor of Gustavo Gutiérrez*, New York: Orbis.

Clark, Bishop Matthew H. (1997) 'The Pastoral Exercise of Authority', *New Theology Review*, August.

Collins, P. (1997) *Papal Power: A Proposal for Change in Catholicism's Third Millennium*, London: Fount Paperback.

Cooper, N. (1993) *Collaborative Ministry: Communion, Contention, Commitment*, New York: Paulist Press.

Cosgrave, B. (1995) 'Structures of Authority', in Sean McReamoinn (ed.), *Authority in the Church*, Blackrock: Columba Press.

Curtice, J. and Jowell, R. (1997) 'Trust in the Political System', in Roger Jowell et al. (eds), *British Social Attitudes, the 14th Report*, Aldershot: Ashgate Publishing.

Duffy, E. (1997) 'Papal Authority', *Priests and People* 11(8, 9).

Gaillardetz, R. (1997) *Teaching with Authority: A Theology of the Magisterium in the Church*, New York: Michael Glazier.

Greeley, A. and Hout, M. (1997) 'The People Cry Reform', *The Tablet*, 22 March.

Hill, E. (1988) *Ministry and Authority in the Catholic Church*, London: Geoffrey Chapman.

Hypher, P. (1997) 'Authority in the Parish', *Priests and People* 11(8, 9).

Inglehart, R. (1990) *Culture Shift in Advanced Industrial Society*, Princeton: Princeton University Press.

Johnson, E. A. (1992) *She Who Is: The Mystery of God in Feminist Theological Discourse*, New York: Crossroad.

Kelly, K. (1993) 'Do We Believe in a Church of Sinners', *The Way*.

McAleese, M. (1995) 'Living with Authority', Sean MacReamoinn (ed.), *Authority in the Church*, Blackrock: Columba Press.

McLoughlin, D. (1997) 'Tensions, Use and Abuse', *Priests and People*, 11(8, 9).

McRedmond, L. (1995) 'Mosaic or Monolith', in Sean MacReamoinn (ed.), *Authority in the Church*, Blackrock: Columba Press.

Mahoney, J. (1985) 'Theological and Pastoral Reflections', in M. Abrams, D. Gerard and N. Timms (eds), *Values and Social Change in Britain*, Basingstoke: Macmillan.

Marcus, R. (1997) 'Recovering the Ancient Tradition', *Priests and People* 11(8, 9).

Markham, I. (1997) *Shades of Grey: The Pope, Christian Ethics and the Ambiguity of Human Situations*, Inaugural Lecture, Hope University College: Briefing 17 July 1997.

Morris, C. (1997) *Church* (Fall 1997), p. 21. Interview with Charles R. Morris about his study of the American Church, entitled *American Catholic*.

Myers, D. G. (1992) *The Pursuit of Happiness: Who is Happy and Why?*, New York: William Morrow.

O'Brien, J. (1994) *Seeds of a New Church*, Blackrock: Columba Press.

Orsy, L. (1997) 'The Interpreter and His Art', *The Jurist*.

Pieris, A. (1989) 'Human Rights Language and Liberation Theology', in Marc H. Ellis and Otto Maduro (eds), *The Future of Liberation Theology: Essays in Honor of Gustavo Guitiérrez*, New York: Orbis.

Quinn, J. R. (1996) 'The Claims of the Primary and the Costly Call to Unity', Lecture on the Occasion of the Centennial of Campion Hall, Oxford.

Reese, T. J. (1996) *Inside the Vatican: The Politics and Organisation of the Catholic Church*, Cambridge, MA: Harvard University Press.

Ryan, D. (1996) *The Catholic Parish: Institutional Discipline, Tribal Identity and Religious Development in the English Church*, London: Sheed and Ward.

Sullivan, F. (1996) *Creative Fidelity: Weighting and Interpreting Documents of the Magisterium*, Dublin: Gill and Macmillan.

Tannen, D. (1986) *That's Not What I Meant*, New York: Ballantine.

Tannen, D. (1990) *You Just Don't Understand*, New York: William Morrow.

Tannen, D. (1994) *Talking From 9 to 5*, New York: William Morrow.

Wilfred, F. (1993) *Beyond Settled Foundations: The Journey of Indian Theology*, Trichy: Department of Christian Studies, University of Madras.

FURTHER READING

compiled by Gerard Mannion

Gerard Mannion is lecturer in Systematic Theology and
Ecclesiology at Trinity and All Saints, Leeds.

Authority and Governance: Philosophical, Political and Social Perspectives

De George, Richard T., *The Nature and Limits of Authority* (Kansas: University Press of Kansas, 1995). Interpreting the nature of authority from the perspective of political philosophy.

Dominian, Jack, *Authority: A Christian Interpretation of the Psychological Evolution of Authority* (London: Darton, Longman and Todd, 1976). A study in the psychological functions of authority and how this relates to the Church.

Heelas, Paul, *Decentralisation: Critical Reflections on Authority and Identity* (Oxford: Blackwell, 1996). Lancaster's Professor of Religion and Modernity offers a 'postmodern' perspective on the central issues of the debate.

Raz, Joseph, *Authority* (Oxford: Blackwell, 1990). Fast becoming a modern classic in political and legal philosophy.

The Teaching Office, Dialogue and Dissent: Debate within the Roman Catholic Church

Curran, Charles E. and McCormick, Richard A. (eds), *Dissent in the Church* (New York: Paulist Press, 1988); and *The Magisterium and Morality* (New York: Paulist Press, 1982). Two invaluable collections of readings which illustrate a diverse range of attitudes to authority and governance in the contemporary Roman Catholic Church.

Gaillardetz, Richard R., *Teaching with Authority* (Collegeville: Liturgical Press, 1997). This recent American study has stimulated debate far beyond the Church in the USA.

Küng, Hans, *Infallible? An Unresolved Enquiry* (1994) (rev. edn. London: SCM). Now a classic study and instrumental in leading the Vatican to deprive its author of his licence to teach as a *Catholic* theologian, this revised edition seeks to bring the original thesis up to date in the light of subsequent ecclesiological developments.

Lash, Nicholas, *Voices of Authority* (London: Sheed and Ward, 1976). An informative analysis of the problem from the former Northampton diocesan priest and recently retired Norris-Hulse Professor of Divinity in the University of Cambridge.

Lefébure, Marcus, Metz, Johann Baptist and Schillebeeckx, Edward (eds), *The Teaching Authority of Believers* (*Concilium*, Edinburgh: T. & T. Clark, 1985). Studies in the relationship between the laity and the Magisterium from the journal concerned with implementing the vision set out at the Second Vatican Council.

Loisy, Alfred F., *The Gospel and the Church* (London: Pitman, 1908). The classic work which served to ignite the Catholic Modernist 'crisis' at the beginning of the twentieth century. Almost one hundred years on, it remains a work of incredible relevance to the difficult debates within the Church today.

MacReamoinn, Sean (ed.), *Authority in the Church* (Blackrock: Columba Press, 1995). An insightful study from the perspective of the Irish church.

Rahner, Karl, 'The Teaching Office of the Church in the Present-Day Crisis of Authority', in *Theological Investigations*, vol. 12 (London: Darton, Longman and Todd, 1974). An excellent assessment of the problem from the Jesuit who both suffered at the hands of the church authorities and helped shape the more progressive vision which emerged from the Second Vatican Council.

Sullivan, Frank A., *Magisterium* (Dublin: Gill and Macmillan, 1983). A well-balanced study which nonetheless demonstrates that canon law and official doctrine is often on the side of the progressives.

Witham, Larry, *Curran versus the Catholic University: A Study of Authority and Freedom in Conflict* (Riverdale: Edington-Rand, 1991). Analyses the backlash against Curran's theology by the Vatican and his erstwhile employers, which led to his removal from the Catholic University of America.

Governance in the Roman Catholic Church

Buckley, M. J., *Papal Primacy and the Episcopate* (New York: Crossroad, 1998). The Jesuit Professor of Systematics from Boston College offers some pertinent observations upon the unresolved problem of collegiality.

Collins, P., *Papal Power: Proposals for Change in the Earth's Third Millennium* (London: Fount, 1997). Positive, progressive and occasionally provocative suggestions from one of the latest individuals to fall foul of the Congregation for the Doctrine of the Faith.

Granfield, Patrick, *The Limits of the Papacy: Authority and Autonomy in the Church* (New York: Crossroad, 1987). An attempt to confront the problem by seeking to define the parameters of authority within the Church.

MacEoin, Gary (ed.), *The Papacy and the People of God* (Maryvale: Orbis, 1999). A very recent collection of essays offering a variety of interpretations concerning the present shape of the Church and its possible future orientation.

Provost, James H. and Knut, Ralf (eds), *The Tabu of Democracy within the Church* (*Concilium*, London: SCM, 1992/5). Studies into the contentious subject of democratic rights and representation in the Church.

Zagano, Phyllis and Tilley, Terence W. (eds), *The Exercise of the Primacy* (New York: Crossroad, 1998). An important collection of essays in response to Archbishop Quinn's lecture at Campion Hall, Oxford on the relationship between the Pope and the bishops of the Church.

Authority, Governance and Ecclesiology

Boff, Leonardo, *Church, Charism and Power* (London: SCM, 1985). A critical study combined with a new vision for the Church from this key figure in liberation theology. This work led to his 'silencing' by the Vatican, as evaluated in the following work.

Cox, Harvey, *The Silencing of Leonardo Boff* (London: Collins, 1989). An insightful study of the issues of authority and governance and the future of Catholicism undertaken by focusing upon Boff as a case study of progressive theology and Ratzinger as a parallel figure from the conservative standpoint.

Hegy, P. (ed.), *The Church in the Nineties: Its Legacy, Its Future* (Collegeville: Liturgical Press, 1993). A collection of essays offering perspectives upon why the Church is undergoing its current difficulties and how it might resolve them.

Küng, H., *The Church* (London: Search Press, 1971). The comprehensive and progressive study in ecclesiology which also fell foul of the Vatican machinery.

Rahner, Karl, *Concern for the Church* (vol. 20 of *Theological Investigations*, London: Darton, Longman and Todd, 1981). The great Jesuit professor's writings upon ecclesiological issues prominent towards the last years of his life.

Rosmini, Antonio, *The Five Wounds of the Church* (Leominster: Fowler Wright, 1987). This classic and prophetic nineteenth-century study continues to hold much relevance today by strength of the insight and vision contained therein. The work proved to be influential upon the young Angelo Roncalli, later to be the 'Pope of the Council' – John XXIII.

Schindler, D. C., *Heart of the World, Centre of the Church* (Edinburgh: T. & T. Clark, 1996). A study into the relationship between the prevailing conservative 'Communio' ecclesiology and more progressive/radical-ecclesiologies.

Authority and Ecumenism in the Christian Church

(Chadwick, Henry), *Christian Authority: Essays in Honour of Henry Chadwick*, ed. Gillian R. Evans (Oxford: Clarendon, 1988). A collection of studies to commemorate the ecumenical contribution of the Cambridge Regius Professor Emeritus of Divinity towards resolving Anglican–Roman Catholic divisions on authority.

Moltmann, Jürgen, Küng, Hans and Lefébure, Marcus (eds), *Who Has the Say in the Church?* (*Concilium*, Edinburgh, T. & T. Clark, 1981). Important essays concerning the very nature and scope of dialogue and debate within the Church.

Yarnold, Edward and Chadwick, Henry, *Truth and Authority* (London: CTS/SPCK, 1977). The ecumenical commentary upon the ARCIC discussions upon authority held in Benice, 1976.

Moral Aspects

Airaksinen, T., *The Ethics of Coercion and Authority* (Pittsburgh: University of Pittsburgh, 1988). A study into the morality of enforcement and authoritarianism.

Curran, Charles E., *Contraception: Authority and Dissent* (London: Burns and Oates, 1969). The seminal work from the moral theologian who helped lead the reaction against *Humanae Vitae* in the United States.

Stout, Jeffrey, *The Flight from Authority* (Notre Dame: University of Notre Dame Press, 1995). A welcome attempt not just to discern the interrelationship of religion and authority, but also to illuminate the *moral* dimension of that relationship.

INDEX